enVisionmath 2.0

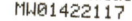

Volume 1A Topics 1-3

Authors

Randall I. Charles
Professor Emeritus
Department of Mathematics
San Jose State University
San Jose, California

Jennifer Bay-Williams
Professor of Mathematics Education
College of Education and Human Development
University of Louisville
Louisville, Kentucky

Robert Q. Berry, III
Associate Professor of Mathematics Education
Department of Curriculum, Instruction and Special Education
University of Virginia
Charlottesville, Virginia

Janet H. Caldwell
Professor of Mathematics
Rowan University
Glassboro, New Jersey

Zachary Champagne
Assistant in Research
Florida Center for Research in Science, Technology, Engineering, and Mathematics (FCR-STEM)
Jacksonville, Florida

Juanita Copley
Professor Emerita, College of Education
University of Houston
Houston, Texas

Warren Crown
Professor Emeritus of Mathematics Education
Graduate School of Education
Rutgers University
New Brunswick, New Jersey

Francis (Skip) Fennell
L. Stanley Bowlsbey Professor of Education and Graduate and Professional Studies
McDaniel College
Westminster, Maryland

Karen Karp
Professor of Mathematics Education
Department of Early Childhood and Elementary Education
University of Louisville
Louisville, Kentucky

Stuart J. Murphy
Visual Learning Specialist
Boston, Massachusetts

Jane F. Schielack
Professor of Mathematics
Associate Dean for Assessment and Pre K-12 Education, College of Science
Texas A&M University
College Station, Texas

Jennifer M. Suh
Associate Professor for Mathematics Education
George Mason University
Fairfax, Virginia

Jonathan A. Wray
Mathematics Instructional Facilitator
Howard County Public Schools
Ellicott City, Maryland

SAVVAS
LEARNING COMPANY

Mathematicians

Roger Howe
Professor of Mathematics
Yale University
New Haven, Connecticut

Gary Lippman
Professor of Mathematics and
Computer Science
California State University, East Bay
Hayward, California

ELL Consultants

Janice R. Corona
Independent Education Consultant
Dallas, Texas

Jim Cummins
Professor
The University of Toronto
Toronto, Canada

Debbie Crisco
Math Coach
Beebe Public Schools
Beebe, Arkansas

Kathleen A. Cuff
Teacher
Kings Park Central School District
Kings Park, New York

Erika Doyle
Math and Science Coordinator
Richland School District
Richland, Washington

Reviewers

Susan Jarvis
Math and Science Curriculum Coordinator
Ocean Springs Schools
Ocean Springs, Mississippi

Copyright © 2017 by Savvas Learning Company LLC. All Rights Reserved. Printed in the United States of America.

This publication is protected by copyright, and permission should be obtained from the publisher prior to any prohibited reproduction, storage in a retrieval system, or transmission in any form or by any means, electronic, mechanical, photocopying, recording, or otherwise. For information regarding permissions, request forms, and the appropriate contacts within the Savvas Learning Company Rights Management group, please send your query to the address below.

Savvas Learning Company LLC, 15 East Midland Avenue, Paramus, NJ 07652

Savvas™ and **Savvas Learning Company™** are the exclusive trademarks of Savvas Learning Company LLC in the U.S. and other countries.

Savvas Learning Company publishes through its famous imprints **Prentice Hall®** and **Scott Foresman®** which are exclusive registered trademarks owned by Savvas Learning Company LLC in the U.S. and/or other countries.

enVisionMATH® and **Savvas Realize™** are exclusive trademarks of Savvas Learning Company LLC in the U.S. and/or other countries.

Unless otherwise indicated herein, any third party trademarks that may appear in this work are the property of their respective owners, and any references to third party trademarks, logos, or other trade dress are for demonstrative or descriptive purposes only. Such references are not intended to imply any sponsorship, endorsement, authorization, or promotion of Savvas Learning Company products by the owners of such marks, or any relationship between the owner and Savvas Learning Company LLC or its authors, licensees, or distributors.

SAVVAS
LEARNING COMPANY

ISBN-13: 978-0-328-93062-3
ISBN-10: 0-328-93062-8
6 2022

You'll be using these digital resources throughout the year!

Digital Resources

Go to SavvasRealize.com

MP
Math Practices Animations to play anytime

Glossary
Animated Glossary in English and Spanish

Help
Another Look Homework Video for extra help

ACTIVe-book
Student Edition online for showing your work

Solve
Solve & Share problems plus math tools

Tools
Math Tools to help you understand

Games
Math Games to help you learn

Learn
Visual Learning Animation Plus with animation, interaction, and math tools

Assessment
Quick Check for each lesson

eText
Student Edition online

SAVVAS realize. Everything you need for math anytime, anywhere

F3

Contents

KEY

- 🟢 Operations and Algebra
- 🔵 Numbers and Computation
- 🔴 Measurement and Data
- 🟡 Geometry

Digital Resources at SavvasRealize.com

TOPICS

1. Solve Addition and Subtraction Problems to 10
2. Fluently Add and Subtract Within 10
3. Addition Facts to 20: Use Strategies
4. Subtraction Facts to 20: Use Strategies
5. Work with Addition and Subtraction Equations
6. Represent and Interpret Data
7. Extend the Counting Sequence
8. Understand Place Value
9. Compare Two-Digit Numbers
10. Use Models and Strategies to Add Tens and Ones
11. Use Models and Strategies to Subtract Tens
12. Measure Lengths
13. Time
14. Reason with Shapes and Their Attributes
15. Equal Shares of Circles and Rectangles

And remember your eText is available at SavvasRealize.com!

TOPIC 1
Solve Addition and Subtraction Problems to 10

Math and Science Project.. 1
Review What You Know.. 2
Vocabulary Cards... 3

1-1	Solve Problems: Add To...................................	9
1-2	Solve Problems: Put Together.............................	15
1-3	Solve Problems: Both Addends Unknown.....................	21
1-4	Solve Problems: Take From................................	27
1-5	Solve Problems: Compare Situations.......................	33
1-6	Continue to Solve Problems: Compare Situations...........	39
1-7	Practice Solving Problems: Add To........................	45
1-8	Solve Problems: Put Together/Take Apart..................	51
1-9	**PROBLEM SOLVING** Construct Arguments..................	57

Fluency Practice Activity.. 63
Vocabulary Review.. 64
Reteaching... 65
Topic Assessment... 69
Topic Performance Assessment... 73

This shows how you can add the parts to find the sum.

4 + 2 =

TOPIC 2
Fluently Add and Subtract Within 10

Math and Science Project.. 75
Review What You Know... 76
Vocabulary Cards.. 77

2-1	Count On to Add 79
2-2	Doubles 85
2-3	Near Doubles 91
2-4	Facts with 5 on a Ten-Frame 97
2-5	Add in Any Order 103
2-6	Count Back to Subtract 109
2-7	Think Addition to Subtract 115
2-8	Continue to Think Addition to Subtract 121
2-9	Solve Word Problems with Facts to 10 127
2-10	**PROBLEM SOLVING** Look For and Use Structure 133

Fluency Practice Activity... 139
Vocabulary Review... 140
Reteaching.. 141
Topic Assessment.. 145
Topic Performance Assessment.. 149

You can think addition to subtract.

7

$7 - 3 = \boxed{?}$

$3 + \boxed{?} = 7$

Contents

SavvasRealize.com

F7

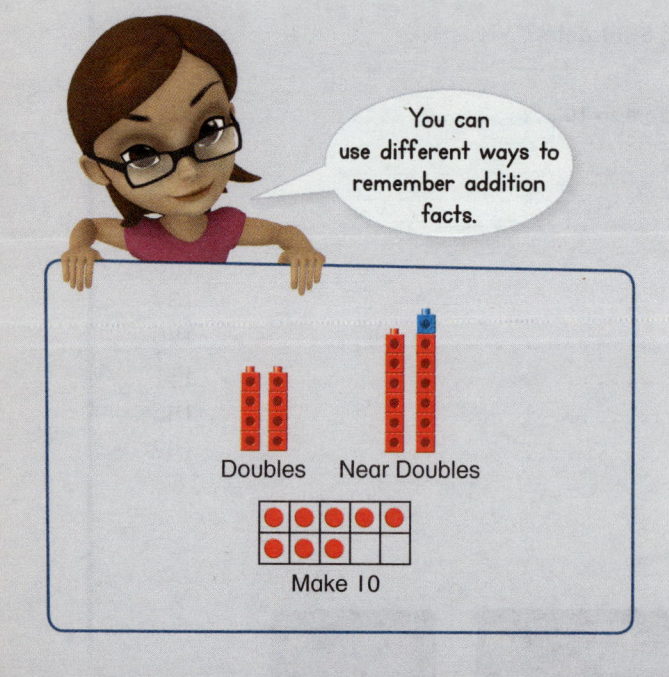

TOPIC 3
Addition Facts to 20: Use Strategies

Math and Science Project.. 151
Review What You Know... 152
Vocabulary Cards... 153

3-1	Count On to Add 155
3-2	Count On to Add Using an Open Number Line 161
3-3	Doubles 167
3-4	Doubles Plus 1 173
3-5	Doubles Plus 2 179
3-6	Make 10 to Add 185
3-7	Continue to Make 10 to Add 191
3-8	Explain Addition Strategies 197
3-9	Solve Addition Word Problems with Facts to 20 203
3-10	PROBLEM SOLVING Critique Reasoning 209

Fluency Practice Activity.. 215
Vocabulary Review.. 216
Reteaching... 217
Topic Assessment... 221
Topic Performance Assessment... 225

You can use different ways to remember addition facts.

Doubles   Near Doubles

Make 10

TOPIC 4
Subtraction Facts to 20: Use Strategies

Math and Science Project.. 227
Review What You Know.. 228
Vocabulary Cards... 229

- **4-1** Count to Subtract.. 231
- **4-2** Make 10 to Subtract.. 237
- **4-3** Continue to Make 10 to Subtract.................... 243
- **4-4** Fact Families.. 249
- **4-5** Use Addition to Subtract................................ 255
- **4-6** Continue to Use Addition to Subtract............ 261
- **4-7** Explain Subtraction Strategies....................... 267
- **4-8** Solve Word Problems with Facts to 20.......... 273
- **4-9** PROBLEM SOLVING Reasoning...................... 279

Fluency Practice Activity... 285
Vocabulary Review... 286
Reteaching... 287
Topic Assessment... 291
Topic Performance Assessment... 295

You can count back to solve subtraction problems.

$10 - 3 = 7$

TOPIC 5
Work with Addition and Subtraction Equations

Math and Science Project... 297
Review What You Know.. 298

5-1	Find the Unknown Numbers........................... 299
5-2	True or False Equations................................... 305
5-3	Make True Equations....................................... 311
5-4	Word Problems with Three Addends............... 317
5-5	Add Three Numbers... 323
5-6	Solve Addition and Subtraction Word Problems.... 329
5-7	**PROBLEM SOLVING** Precision.. 335

Fluency Practice Activity... 341
Vocabulary Review.. 342
Reteaching.. 343
Topic Assessment... 345
Topic Performance Assessment................................ 347

You can add three numbers in different ways.

TOPIC 6
Represent and Interpret Data

Math and Science Project.. 349
Review What You Know... 350
Vocabulary Cards.. 351

6-1 Organize Data into Three Categories............................ 353

6-2 Collect and Represent Data.. 359

6-3 Interpret Data... 365

6-4 Continue to Interpret Data... 371

6-5 PROBLEM SOLVING
Make Sense and Persevere.. 377

Fluency Practice Activity.. 383
Vocabulary Review... 384
Reteaching.. 385
Topic Assessment... 387
Topic Performance Assessment.. 389

You can show data in a tally chart.

Contents

F11

TOPIC 7
Extend the Counting Sequence

Math and Science Project.. 391
Review What You Know.. 392
Vocabulary Cards.. 393

7-1 Count by 10s to 120 395

7-2 Count by 1s to 120 401

7-3 Count on a Number Chart to 120 407

7-4 Count by 1s or 10s to 120 413

7-5 Count on an Open Number Line 419

7-6 Count and Write Numerals 425

7-7 PROBLEM SOLVING
Repeated Reasoning 431

Fluency Practice Activity.. 437
Vocabulary Review... 438
Reteaching... 439
Topic Assessment 441
Topic Performance Assessment............................. 443

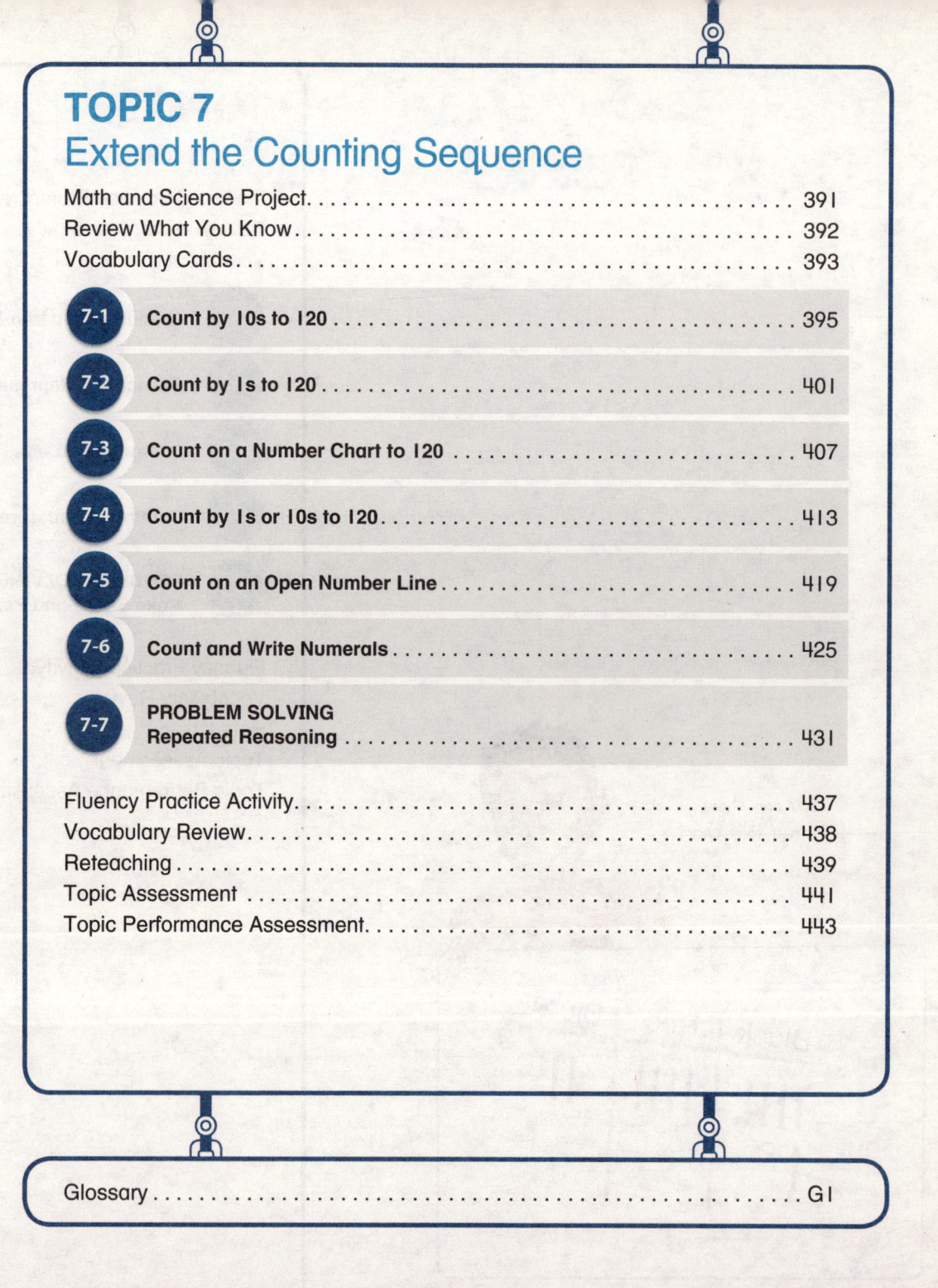

Glossary.. G1

Counting above 100 is just like counting below 100.

100, 101

TOPIC 8 in Volume 2
Understand Place Value

Math and Science Project..........................445
Review What You Know............................446
Vocabulary Cards................................447

8-1	Make Numbers 11 to 19..........................449
8-2	Numbers Made with Tens.........................455
8-3	Count with Groups of Tens and Leftovers.........461
8-4	Tens and Ones..................................467
8-5	Continue with Tens and Ones....................473
8-6	PROBLEM SOLVING Look For and Use Structure...479

Fluency Practice Activity........................485
Vocabulary Review................................486
Reteaching.......................................487
Topic Assessment.................................489
Topic Performance Assessment.....................491

TOPIC 9 in Volume 2
Compare Two-Digit Numbers

Math and Science Project..........................493
Review What You Know............................494
Vocabulary Cards................................495

9-1	1 More, 1 Less; 10 More, 10 Less...............497
9-2	Make Numbers on a Hundred Chart................503
9-3	Compare Numbers................................509
9-4	Compare Numbers with Symbols (>, <, =).........515
9-5	Compare Numbers on a Number Line...............521
9-6	PROBLEM SOLVING Make Sense and Persevere....527

Fluency Practice Activity........................533
Vocabulary Review................................534
Reteaching.......................................535
Topic Assessment.................................537
Topic Performance Assessment.....................539

TOPIC 10 in Volume 2
Use Models and Strategies to Add Tens and Ones

Math and Science Project................................. 541
Review What You Know.................................. 542

- **10-1** Add Tens Using Models............................ 543
- **10-2** Mental Math: Ten More Than a Number.......... 549
- **10-3** Add Tens and Ones Using a Hundred Chart...... 555
- **10-4** Add Tens and Ones Using an Open Number Line... 561
- **10-5** Add Tens and Ones Using Models................. 567
- **10-6** Make a Ten to Add................................ 573
- **10-7** Add Using Place Value............................ 579
- **10-8** Practice Adding Using Strategies................. 585
- **10-9** PROBLEM SOLVING
  Model with Math................................... 591

Fluency Practice Activity................................... 597
Vocabulary Review... 598
Reteaching... 599
Topic Assessment.. 603
Topic Performance Assessment............................ 607

TOPIC 11 in Volume 2
Use Models and Strategies to Subtract Tens

Math and Science Project................................. 609
Review What You Know.................................. 610

- **11-1** Subtract Tens Using Models...................... 611
- **11-2** Subtract Tens Using a Hundred Chart............ 617
- **11-3** Subtract Tens Using an Open Number Line....... 623
- **11-4** Use Addition to Subtract Tens.................... 629
- **11-5** Mental Math: Ten Less Than a Number........... 635
- **11-6** Use Strategies to Practice Subtraction........... 641
- **11-7** PROBLEM SOLVING
  Model with Math................................... 647

Fluency Practice Activity................................... 653
Vocabulary Review... 654
Reteaching... 655
Topic Assessment.. 657
Topic Performance Assessment............................ 659

TOPIC 12 in Volume 2
Measure Lengths

Math and Science Project..................................661
Review What You Know....................................662
Vocabulary Cards..663

12-1 Compare and Order by Length......................667

12-2 Indirect Measurement.............................673

12-3 Use Units to Measure Length.....................679

12-4 Continue to Measure Length......................685

12-5 PROBLEM SOLVING
Use Appropriate Tools.....................691

Fluency Practice Activity................................697
Vocabulary Review..698
Reteaching...699
Topic Assessment...701
Topic Performance Assessment.............................703

TOPIC 13 in Volume 2
Time

Math and Science Project..................................705
Review What You Know....................................706
Vocabulary Cards..707

13-1 Understand the Hour and Minute Hands............709

13-2 Tell and Write Time to the Hour.................715

13-3 Tell and Write Time to the Half Hour............721

13-4 PROBLEM SOLVING
Reasoning.................................727

Fluency Practice Activity................................733
Vocabulary Review..734
Reteaching...735
Topic Assessment...737
Topic Performance Assessment.............................739

TOPIC 14 in Volume 2
Reason with Shapes and Their Attributes

Math and Science Project.. 741
Review What You Know.. 742
Vocabulary Cards.. 743

- **14-1** Use Attributes to Define Two-Dimensional (2-D) Shapes 747
- **14-2** Defining and Non-Defining Attributes of 2-D Shapes 753
- **14-3** Build and Draw 2-D Shapes by Attributes 759
- **14-4** Compose 2-D Shapes 765
- **14-5** Compose New 2-D Shapes from 2-D Shapes 771
- **14-6** Use Attributes to Define Three-Dimensional (3-D) Shapes 777
- **14-7** Defining and Non-Defining Attributes of 3-D Shapes 783
- **14-8** Compose with 3-D Shapes..................................... 789
- **14-9** PROBLEM SOLVING
  Make Sense and Persevere 795

Fluency Practice Activity... 801
Vocabulary Review... 802
Reteaching... 803
Topic Assessment.. 807
Topic Performance Assessment.. 811

TOPIC 15 in Volume 2
Equal Shares of Circles and Rectangles

Math and Science Project.. 813
Review What You Know.. 814
Vocabulary Cards.. 815

- **15-1** Make Equal Shares 817
- **15-2** Make Halves and Fourths of Rectangles and Circles 823
- **15-3** Understand Halves and Fourths 829
- **15-4** PROBLEM SOLVING
  Model with Math 835

Fluency Practice Activity... 841
Vocabulary Review... 842
Reteaching... 843
Topic Assessment.. 845
Topic Performance Assessment.. 847

STEP UP to Grade 2 in Volume 2

Step Up Opener 849

1. Even and Odd Numbers 851
2. Use Arrays to Find Totals 855
3. Add on a Hundred Chart 859
4. Models to Add 2-Digit Numbers 863
5. Subtract on a Hundred Chart 867
6. Models to Subtract 2- and 1-Digit Numbers 871
7. Tell Time to Five Minutes 875
8. Understand Hundreds 879
9. Counting Hundreds, Tens, and Ones 883
10. Skip Count by 5, 10, and 100, to 1,000 887

Glossary G1

These lessons help prepare you for Grade 2.

Problem Solving Handbook

Math practices are ways we think about and do math.

Math practices will help you solve problems.

Problem Solving Handbook

Math Practices

1. Make sense of problems and persevere in solving them.

2. Reason abstractly and quantitatively.

3. Construct viable arguments and critique the reasoning of others.

4. Model with mathematics.

5. Use appropriate tools strategically.

6. Attend to precision.

7. Look for and make use of structure.

8. Look for and express regularity in repeated reasoning.

There are good Thinking Habits for each of these math practices.

1. Make sense of problems and persevere in solving them.

Good math thinkers know what the problem is about. They have a plan to solve it. They keep trying if they get stuck.

My plan was to find all the ways 9 counters can be put into 2 groups.

What pairs of numbers from 0 to 9 add to 9?

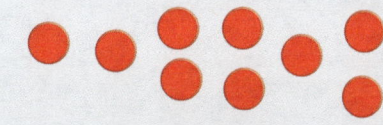

0 + 9 = 9
1 + 8 = 9
2 + 7 = 9

Thinking Habits

What do I need to find?

What do I know?

What's my plan for solving the problem?

What else can I try if I get stuck?

How can I check that my solution makes sense?

Problem Solving Handbook

2 Reason abstractly and quantitatively.

I thought about what numbers would make 8. I used an equation with those numbers to show the problem.

Good math thinkers know how to think about words and numbers to solve problems.

Alan has 8 blue marbles.
He wants to give them to Tom and Rosi.
How can Alan break apart the 8 blue marbles?

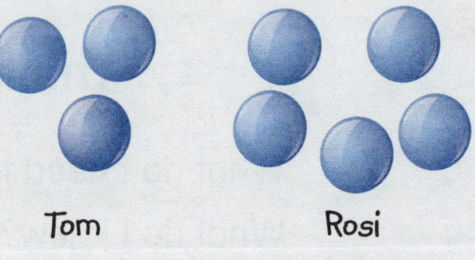

Tom   Rosi

$8 = 3 + 5$

Thinking Habits

What do the numbers stand for?

How are the numbers in the problem related?

How can I show a word problem using pictures or numbers?

How can I use a word problem to show what an equation means?

3 Construct viable arguments and critique the reasoning of others.

"I used a picture and words to explain my thinking."

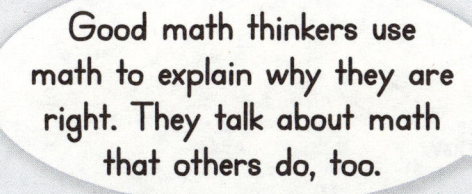

"Good math thinkers use math to explain why they are right. They talk about math that others do, too."

Joan has 7 pencils. Sam has 9 pencils. Who has more pencils? Show how you know.

I drew pencils for Joan and for Sam. I matched up the pencils. Sam has more pencils than Joan.

Joan's pencils | | | | | | | |
Sam's pencils | | | | | | | | | |

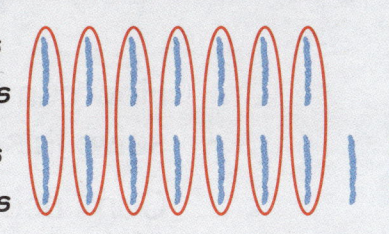

Thinking Habits

How can I use math to explain my work?

Am I using numbers and symbols correctly?

Is my explanation clear?

What questions can I ask to understand other people's thinking?

Are there mistakes in other people's thinking?

Can I improve other people's thinking?

Problem Solving Handbook

4 Model with mathematics.

"I used ten-frames to show the problem."

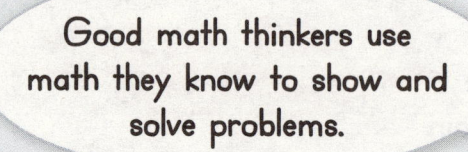

"Good math thinkers use math they know to show and solve problems."

Ali collects rocks. He puts 17 rocks in boxes. Each box holds 10 rocks. He fills 1 box. How many rocks are in the second box?

Thinking Habits

How can I use the math I know to help solve this problem?

Can I use a drawing, diagram, table, graph, or objects to show the problem?

Can I write an equation to show the problem?

5. Use appropriate tools strategically.

"I chose to use cubes to solve the problem."

"Good math thinkers know how to pick the right tools to solve math problems."

Ed finds 5 nuts on a tree. He finds 4 more nuts in the grass. How many nuts does Ed find?

Thinking Habits

Which tools can I use?

Is there a different tool I could use?

Am I using the tool correctly?

6 Attend to precision.

"I used math words correctly to write what I noticed."

"Good math thinkers are careful about what they write and say, so their ideas about math are clear."

How are these shapes alike?

They have 4 sides.
They have 4 corners.
They have straight sides.

Thinking Habits

Am I using numbers, units, and symbols correctly?

Am I using the correct definitions?

Is my answer clear?

Problem Solving Handbook

7 Look for and make use of structure.

"I found a pattern."

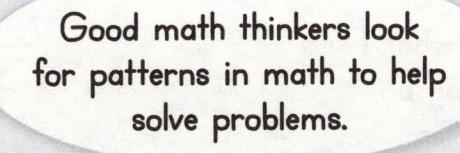

"Good math thinkers look for patterns in math to help solve problems."

What are the next two numbers? Fill in the blanks. Explain and show your thinking.

15, 16, 17, 18, 19, _____, _____

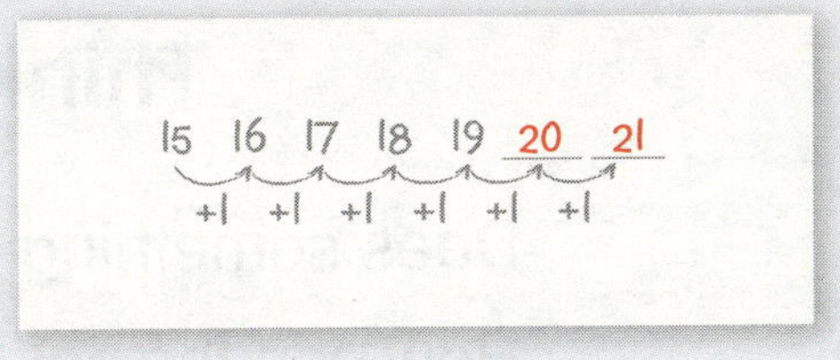

15 16 17 18 19 20 21
 +1 +1 +1 +1 +1 +1

Thinking Habits

Is there a pattern?

How can I describe the pattern?

Can I break the problem into simpler parts?

Problem Solving Handbook

Look for and express regularity in repeated reasoning.

MP 8

"Each new person has 1 more box. I used what I know about counting on to solve this problem."

"Good math thinkers look for things that repeat in a problem. They use what they learn from one problem to help them solve other problems."

Jay has 3 boxes.
Nicole has 1 more box than Jay.
Krista has 1 more box than Nicole.
How many boxes does Nicole have?
How many boxes does Krista have? Explain.

☐ ☐ ☐

1 more than 3 is 4.
Nicole has 4 boxes.
1 more than 4 is 5.
Krista has 5 boxes.

Thinking Habits

Does something repeat in the problem?

How can the solution help me solve another problem?

Problem Solving Handbook

Problem Solving Guide

These questions can help you solve problems.

Make Sense of the Problem

Reason
- What do I need to find?
- What given information can I use?
- How are the quantities related?

Think About Similar Problems
- Have I solved problems like this before?

Persevere in Solving the Problem

Model with Math
- How can I use the math I know?
- How can I show the problem?
- Is there a pattern I can use?

Use Appropriate Tools
- What math tools could I use?
- How can I use those tools?

Check the Answer

Make Sense of the Answer
- Is my answer reasonable?

Check for Precision
- Did I check my work?
- Is my answer clear?
- Is my explanation clear?

Some Ways to Show Problems
- Draw a Picture
- Draw a Number Line
- Write an Equation

Some Math Tools
- Objects
- Technology
- Paper and Pencil

Problem Solving Handbook
Problem Solving Recording Sheet

This sheet helps you organize your work.

Name: Ehrin

Teaching Tool 1

Problem Solving Recording Sheet

Problem:
Billy has 8 green marbles and 4 blue marbles. How many marbles does he have in all?

Make 10 to solve.
Show your work.

MAKE SENSE OF THE PROBLEM

Need to Find	Given
I need to find how many marbles Billy has in all.	Billy has 8 green marbles and 4 blue marbles.

PERSEVERE IN SOLVING THE PROBLEM

Some Ways to Represent Problems
- ☑ Draw a Picture
- ☐ Draw a Number Line
- ☑ Write an Equation

Some Math Tools
- ☐ Objects
- ☐ Technology
- ☑ Paper and Pencil

Solution and Answer

●●●●○ ○
●●●●○ ○
 10   2

$8 + 2 = 10$
$10 + 2 = 12$
Billy has 12 marbles.

CHECK THE ANSWER

I counted the counters I drew.
There are 12.
My answer is correct.

TT1

Name _____

Writing Numbers 0 to 4

GRADE 1 Readiness

Practice writing the numbers 0–4.

1. 0 0 0
2. 1 1 1
3. 2 2 2
4. 3 3 3
5. 4 4 4

Grade 1 | Readiness

R1

Writing Numbers 5 to 9

Practice writing the numbers 5–9.

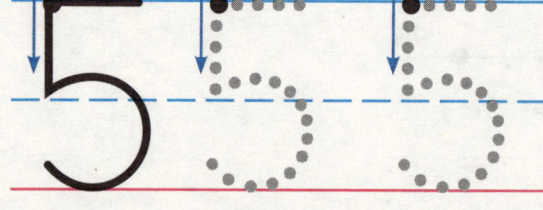

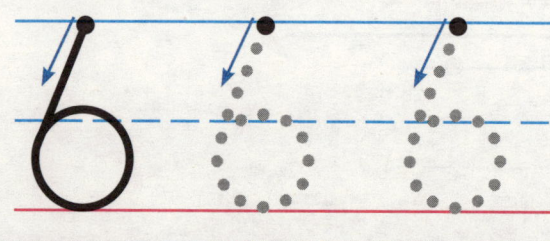

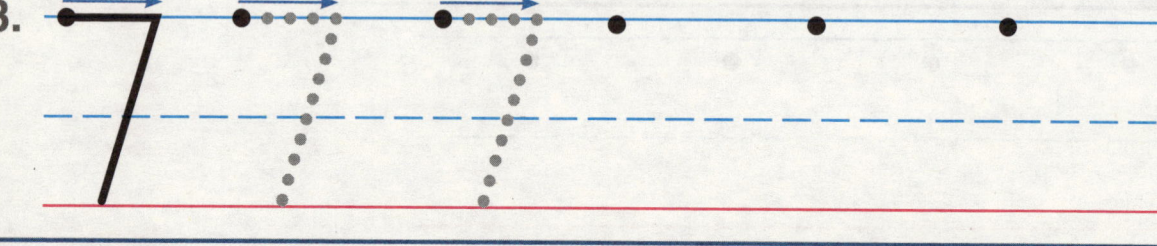

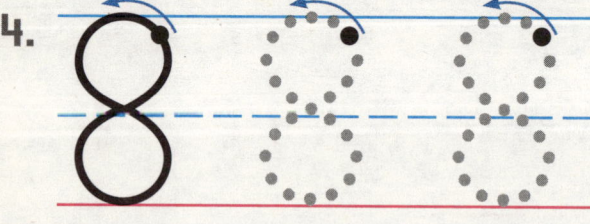

1. 5 5 5
2. 6 6 6
3. 7 7 7
4. 8 8 8
5. 9 9 9

Grade I | Readiness

Name _____

Counting and Writing to 9

Count and write the number of dots.

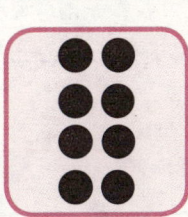

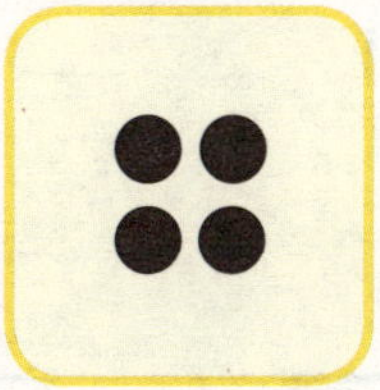

GRADE 1 Readiness

1. 5
2. 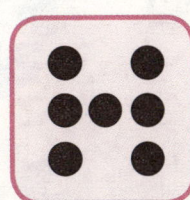 6
3. 3 
4.  9
5. 8
6. 4
7. 6
8. 5
9. 8

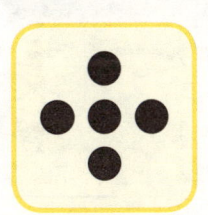

Grade 1 | Readiness

Comparing Numbers Through 5

Write the number that tells how many. Then circle the number that is less.

1. 2 3

2.

3.

4.

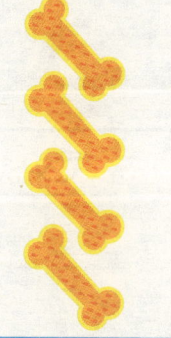

R4 — Copyright © Savvas Learning Company LLC. All Rights Reserved. — Grade 1 | Readiness

Name _____

Comparing Numbers Through 10

Grade 1 Readiness

Write the number that tells how many. Then circle the number that is greater.

1. 7    (8)

2. ____   ____

Making Numbers 6 to 9

Write the number inside and outside. Then write the number in all.

1.  ____ inside   ____ outside   ____ in all

2.  ____ inside   ____ outside   ____ in all

Write the numbers to show the parts.

3. ____ 🔵 and ____ 🟢

4.   ____ 🔵 and ____ 🟢

R6 — Grade 1 | Readiness

Name _____

Finding Missing Parts of Numbers 6 to 9

Readiness — GRADE 1

Find the missing parts. Then write the numbers.

1. 6 bones in all.

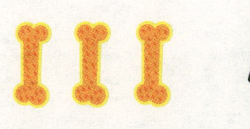

   ___ ___
   part I know   missing part

2. 6 bones in all.

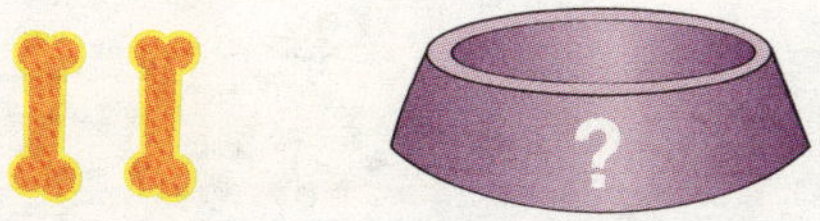

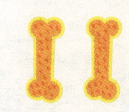

   ___ ___
   part I know   missing part

3. 7 bones in all.

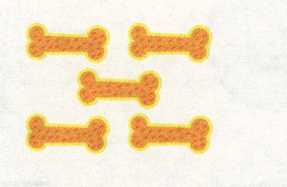

   ___ ___
   part I know   missing part

4. 8

   ___ ___
   part I know   missing part

5. 9

   ___ ___
   part I know   missing part

6. 8

   ___ ___
   part I know   missing part

Find the missing part. Then complete the addition equation.

7. Mark has 9 bagels. He cooks 4 of them. How many bagels are **NOT** cooked?

   $4 + \underline{} = 9$

8. Hanna has 7 eggs. 5 eggs hatched. How many eggs are **NOT** hatched?

   $5 + \underline{} = 7$

Grade 1 | Readiness

Shapes

Color each shape below.

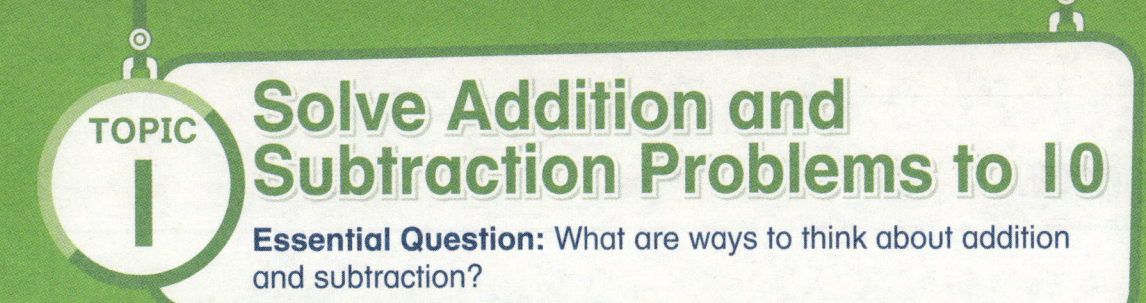

TOPIC 1: Solve Addition and Subtraction Problems to 10

Essential Question: What are ways to think about addition and subtraction?

Look at the adult and baby giraffes.

How are they the same? How are they different?

Wow! Let's do this project and learn more.

Math and Science Project: Parents and Babies

Find Out Talk to friends and relatives about different animals and their babies. Ask them how the parents and babies are the same and how they are different.

Journal: Make a Book Show what you found. In your book, also:
- Draw some animals, including the parents and babies.
- Create and solve addition and subtraction stories about some animals and their babies.

Name _____

Review What You Know

Vocabulary

1. **Count** the fish. Write the number that tells how many.

2. **Join** the two groups and write how many.

3. Write how many soccer balls there are **in all**.

Counting

4. Tammy has 4 balloons. Draw a picture of her balloons.

5. Write the number that tells how many cats.

Sums

6. Circle the number that shows how many crabs you see.

2   3   4   5

My Word Cards Study the words on the front of the card. Complete the activity on the back.

add

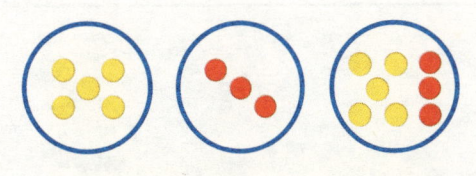

$5 + 3 = 8$

sum

$2 + 3 = 5$
↑
sum

plus

$5 + 4$

5 **plus** 4

This means 4 is added to 5.

equation

$6 + 4 = 10$ $6 - 2 = 4$

$10 = 6 + 4$ $4 = 6 - 2$

$6 + 4 = 8 + 2$

These are **equations**.

equals

$5 = 4 + 1$

5 **equals** 4 plus 1.

$5 + 2 = 7$

5 plus 2 **equals** 7.

part

2 and 3 are parts of 5.

Topic 1 | My Word Cards   three **3**

My Word Cards

Use what you know to complete the sentences.
Extend learning by writing your own sentence using each word.

---

2 _____

2 equal 4.

The answer to an addition equation is called the

_____.

I use a plus sign to

_____.

A _____

is a piece of a whole.

---

4 plus 4

_____ 8.

I can solve a word problem by writing an

_____.

My Word Cards Study the words on the front of the card. Complete the activity on the back.

whole

5

The **whole** is 5.

difference

$4 - 1 = 3$

↑
difference

subtract

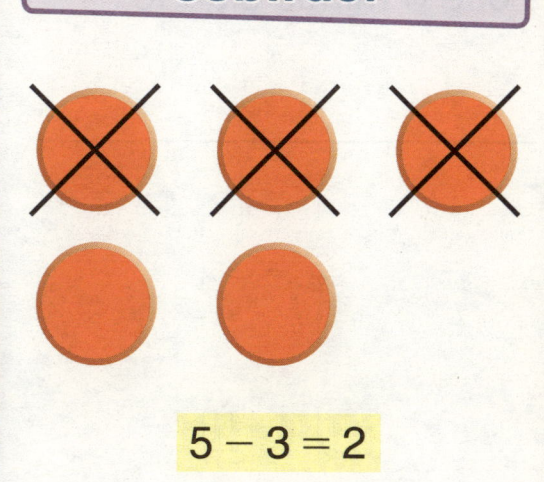

$5 - 3 = 2$

minus

$5 - 3$

5 **minus** 3

This means 3 is taken away from 5.

more

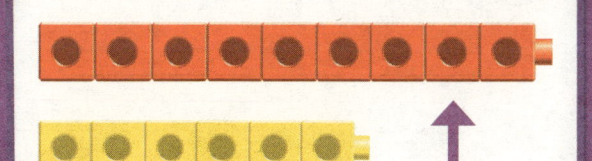

The red row has **more**.

fewer

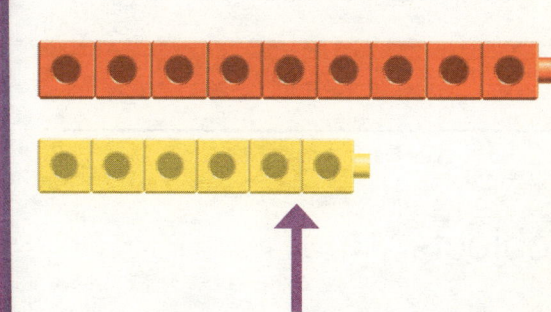

The yellow row has **fewer**.

Topic 1 | My Word Cards   five **5**

My Word Cards

Use what you know to complete the sentences.
Extend learning by writing your own sentence using each word.

I use a minus sign to
_____.

The answer to a subtraction equation is called the
_____.

When I add all of the parts, I make a
_____.

The group that has less has
_____
objects.

The group with a greater number of objects has
_____.

5 _____ 3 equals 2.

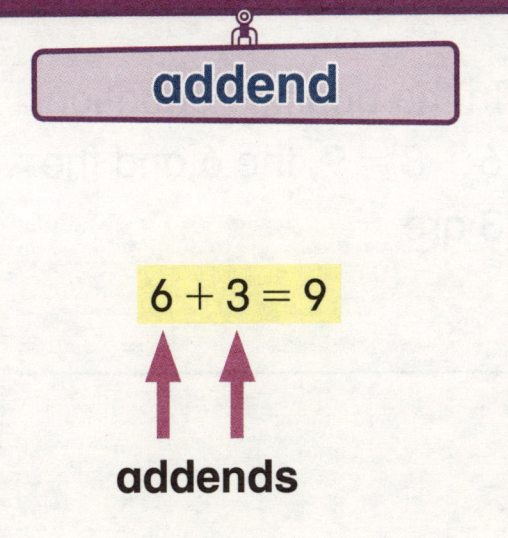

My Word Cards Study the words on the front of the card. Complete the activity on the back.

addend

6 + 3 = 9
↑ ↑
addends

Topic 1 | My Word Cards

seven 7

My Word Cards

Use what you know to complete the sentences. Extend learning by writing your own sentence using each word.

In the addition equation $6 + 3 = 9$, the 6 and the 3 are

_____.

Name _____

Lesson 1-1
Solve Problems: Add To

Solve & Share

Jada has 2 🟥. She adds on 1 more 🟥. How many 🟥 does she have now?

How can you show this story with cubes and an addition equation?

I can ...
solve word problems about adding to.

I can also model with math.

___ + ___ = ___

Topic 1 | Lesson 1

nine 9

Paul has 5 🟦. He snaps on 2 more 🟦. How many 🟦 does he have now?

You can show the problem on a part-part mat.

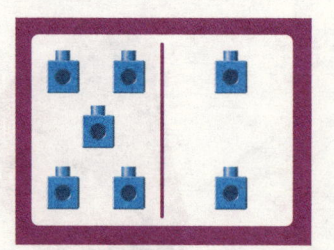

Add to find how many in all.

You can write an addition **equation** to match the problem.

$\underline{5} + \underline{2} = \underline{7}$

I can add to a number to find the sum.

5 plus 2 equals 7. Paul now has 7 🟦.

Do You Understand?

Show Me! You have 4 🟥. You snap on 3 more 🟥. How can you find how many 🟥 you have now?

Guided Practice

Write an addition equation to match each problem. Use the pictures to help you.

1. Warren has 3 🟩. He snaps on 3 more 🟩. How many 🟩 does he have now?

   $\underline{3} + \underline{3} = \underline{6}$

2. Anna has 2 🟠. She buys 6 more 🟠. How many 🟠 does Anna have now?

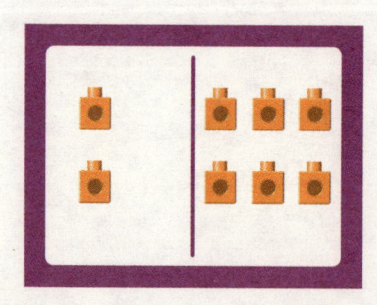

   $\underline{} + \underline{} = \underline{}$

Name _____

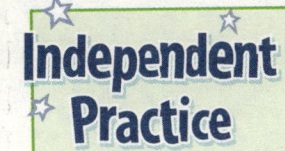

Independent Practice

Write an addition equation to match each problem. Use the pictures to help you.

3. 4 🐝 are in the garden.
   4 more 🐝 join them.
   How many 🐝 are there now?

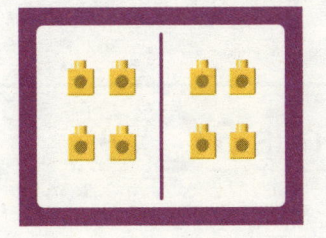

   ___ + ___ = ___

4. 3 🐞 are on a leaf.
   6 more 🐞 join them.
   How many 🐞 are there now?

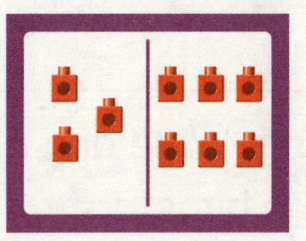

   ___ + ___ = ___

Draw a picture to solve the story problem. Then write an addition equation.

5. **Higher Order Thinking** 6 🦆 are in the pond. 2 more 🦆 join them. 4 🐞 are in the grass. How many 🦆 are in the pond now?

   ___ + ___ = ___

Topic 1 | Lesson 1

eleven 11

Problem Solving Solve each problem below.

6. Vocabulary There are 3 🐰.
4 more 🐰 join them.
How many 🐰 are there now?

Write an addition **equation**.

___ + ___ = ___

7. Model 8 🐱 are playing.
1 more 🐱 joins them.
How many 🐱 are playing now?

Write an addition equation.

___ + ___ = ___

8. Higher Order Thinking Write an addition story about the birds.

Use pictures, numbers, or words.

9. Assessment Lisa has 5 ⚾.
She finds 3 more ⚾.
How many ⚾ does Lisa have now?

Which addition equation matches the story?

Ⓐ $5 + 1 = 6$

Ⓑ $5 + 2 = 7$

Ⓒ $5 + 3 = 8$

Ⓓ $5 + 4 = 9$

12 twelve

Name _____

Homework & Practice 1-1
Solve Problems: Add To

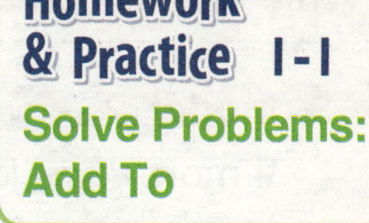

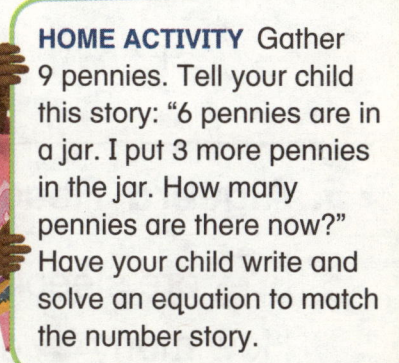

Another Look! You can use addition to solve some word problems.

5 🐰 play in the grass.
3 more 🐰 join them.
How many 🐰 are there now?

$5 + 3 = 8$

7 🐞 are on a leaf.
2 more 🐞 join them.
How many 🐞 are there now?

$\underline{7} + \underline{2} = \underline{9}$

Use color tiles to find the total.

HOME ACTIVITY Gather 9 pennies. Tell your child this story: "6 pennies are in a jar. I put 3 more pennies in the jar. How many pennies are there now?" Have your child write and solve an equation to match the number story.

Write an addition equation to match each problem. Use the pictures to help you.

1. 3 🐸 are in the pond.
   3 more 🐸 join them.
   How many 🐸 are there now?

   ___ + ___ = ___

2. 2 🐞 are on a rock.
   3 more 🐞 join them.
   How many 🐞 are there now?

   ___ + ___ = ___

Topic 1 | Lesson 1   Digital Resources at SavvasRealize.com   thirteen 13

Write an addition equation to solve each problem.

3. **Model** 2 🐭 are sleeping. 4 more 🐭 join them. How many 🐭 are there now?

___ + ___ = ___

4. **Model** 5 ⚽ are on the field. 5 more ⚽ roll on the field. How many ⚽ are on the field now?

___ + ___ = ___

5. **Algebra** Read the story. Write the numbers missing from the equation.

3 🐰 are sleeping. 2 more 🐰 join them. How many 🐰 are there now?

___ + 2 = ___

6. **Higher Order Thinking** Tell an addition story about the frogs. Then write an equation to show how many in all.

___ + ___ = ___

7. **Assessment** Which equation describes the picture?

Ⓐ 3 + 0 = 3
Ⓑ 2 + 2 = 4
Ⓒ 3 + 1 = 4
Ⓓ 3 + 2 = 5

Name _____

Lesson 1-2
Solve Problems: Put Together

I can ...
solve word problems about putting together.

I can also make sense of problems.

Your 2 bags each have connecting cubes of a different color. Pick out a handful of cubes from each bag.

How can you use numbers to show how many cubes you picked in all? Show your work.

Topic 1 | Lesson 2

fifteen 15

Kenny picks 4 🟥 and 2 🟦.

The **parts** are 4 and 2.

$\underline{4} \quad \underline{2}$

Add the parts to find the **whole**.

$\underline{4} + \underline{2} = \underline{}$

Write an addition equation to show the parts and the whole.

$\underline{4} + \underline{2} = \underline{6}$

Kenny picks 6 cubes in all.

I put the parts together when I add.

Do You Understand?

Show Me! You have 2 🟥 and 3 🟦. How can you find how many cubes you have in all?

Guided Practice

Write the parts. Then write an addition equation to match each problem.

1. Cheryl has 3 🟪 and 5 🟩. How many cubes does she have in all?

   $\underline{3} + \underline{5}$
   $\underline{3} + \underline{5} = \underline{8}$

2. Jenny sees 1 🐞 and 6 🐝. How many bugs does Jenny see in all?

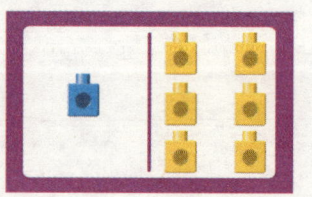

   $\underline{} + \underline{}$
   $\underline{} = \underline{} + \underline{}$

Name _____

Independent Practice — Write the parts. Then write an addition equation to match each problem.

3. The pet store has 3 🐰 and 4 🐱. How many pets does the store have in all?

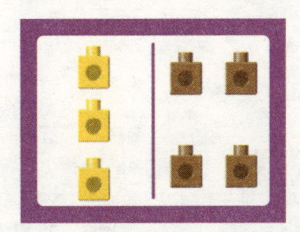

   ___ + ___

   ___ + ___ = ___

4. The box holds 3 ⚾ and 3 ⚽. How many balls are in the box?

   ___ + ___

   ___ + ___ = ___

5. **Higher Order Thinking** Marco finds 2 brown 🪨, 7 red 🪨, and 3 🐚. How many 🪨 did Marco find in all?

   Draw a picture to solve.
   Then write an addition equation.

   ___ + ___ = ___

Topic 1 | Lesson 2

seventeen 17

Problem Solving
Solve each problem below.

6. Make Sense Jen finds 2 🍃. Then she finds 5 more 🍃. How many 🍃 did Jen find?

Draw a picture to show that you know what the story means. Then write an addition equation.

____ + ____ = ____

7. Higher Order Thinking Draw a picture to show an addition story about red worms and brown worms. Write an equation to tell how many worms there are in all.

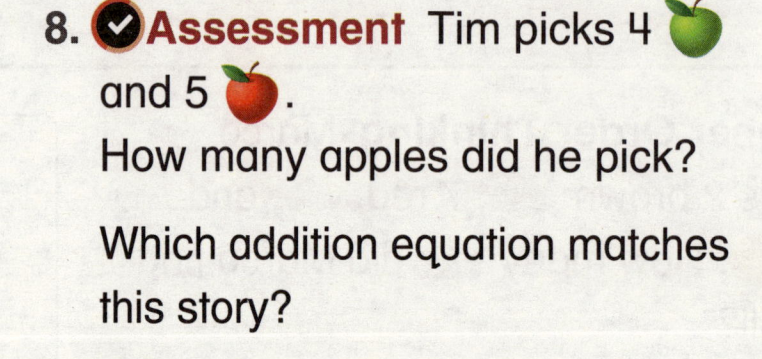

____ = ____ + ____

8. Assessment Tim picks 4 🍏 and 5 🍎. How many apples did he pick?

Which addition equation matches this story?

Ⓐ 9 + 4 = 13
Ⓑ 4 + 5 = 9
Ⓒ 3 + 6 = 9
Ⓓ 4 + 4 = 8

Name _____

Homework & Practice 1-2
Solve Problems: Put Together

Another Look! Use the parts to write an addition equation.

I have 2 red counters and 3 yellow counters. These are the parts. I have 5 counters in all.

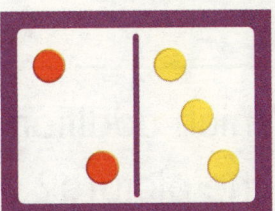

$2 + 3$
$2 + 3 = 5$

Greg has 3 🔴 and 5 🟡. How many counters does he have in all?

$\underline{3} + \underline{5}$
$\underline{3} + \underline{5} = \underline{8}$

HOME ACTIVITY Give your child 2 groups of small objects to count (e.g., one group of 3 buttons and one group of 4 buttons of a different color). Together, find the total number of objects and say the corresponding addition equation (e.g., "3 plus 4 equals 7."). Repeat the activity several times with different groupings.

Write the parts. Then write an addition equation to match each problem.

1. Stephanie has 4 🔴 and 2 🟡. How many counters does she have in all?

   ___ + ___
   ___ + ___ = ___

2. Glen has 4 🔴 and 4 🟡. How many counters does he have in all?

   ___ + ___
   ___ + ___ = ___

Topic 1 | Lesson 2

Write an addition equation for each story.

3. **Model** Ian picks 3 🍎.
Then he picks 5 more 🍎.
How many 🍎 did Ian pick in all?

___ + ___ = ___

4. **Model** Sara has 2 🪨.
Jake has 4 🪨.
How many 🪨 do they have in all?

___ + ___ = ___

5. **Higher Order Thinking** Circle 2 groups of fruit. Write an addition equation to tell how many pieces of fruit there are in your 2 groups.

___ + ___ = ___

6. **Assessment** Which addition equation matches the picture?

Ⓐ $4 + 4 = 8$
Ⓑ $4 + 5 = 9$
Ⓒ $2 + 7 = 9$
Ⓓ $4 + 6 = 10$

Name _____

Lesson 1-3

Solve Problems: Both Addends Unknown

Solve & Share

Show how you could place the 5 pencils in these two cups. Complete the equation to show your work. Then talk to a classmate. Are your equations the same?

I can ...
solve word problems by breaking apart the total number of objects.

I can also make math arguments.

$5 = \underline{} + \underline{}$

Topic 1 | Lesson 3

Digital Resources at SavvasRealize.com

twenty-one **21**

There are 7 penguins. How many can go inside and outside the cave?

Here is one way to show the 7 penguins.

There are still 7 penguins. 4 is one part. 3 is the other part.

You can write an equation to show the whole and the parts.

$7 = 4 + 3$

Here is another way to show the 7 penguins.

$7 = 5 + 2$

Do You Understand?

Show Me! What are two different ways that 4 penguins could be inside or outside the cave?

Guided Practice Draw a picture to show the parts. Then write an equation.

1. There are 5 🐧 in all. How many are inside and outside the cave?

   $5 = 3 + 2$

2. There are 8 🐧 in all. How many are inside and outside the cave?

   ___ = ___ + ___

22 twenty-two

Topic 1 | Lesson 3

Name _____

Independent Practice — Draw pictures to show how many are inside and outside each cave. Then write an equation.

3. There are 9 🕷 in all.

____ = ____ + ____

4. There are 8 🕷 in all.

____ = ____ + ____

5. There are 5 🕷 in all.

____ = ____ + ____

6. There are 7 🕷 in all.

____ = ____ + ____

Topic 1 | Lesson 3

Problem Solving Solve each problem.

7. Math and Science There are 8 monkeys. Some are parents and some are babies. How many of each could there be? Show two different ways.

____ parents and ____ babies

OR

____ parents and ____ babies

8. Reasoning Krista takes 2 photos. Then she takes 5 more. How many photos does Krista take in all? Write an addition equation to show your work.

____ + ____ = ____

____ photos

9. Higher Order Thinking Andy's team scored a total of 10 goals in two games. They scored 1 or 2 goals in the first game. How many goals could they have scored in the second game? Explain how you know.

10. Assessment Jess sees 9 birds. Some are flying and some are sitting in a tree.

Match the number of birds flying with the number of birds Jess could have seen in the tree.

7 flying   3 in the tree
8 flying   1 in the tree
5 flying   2 in the tree
6 flying   4 in the tree

Name _____

Homework & Practice 1-3
Solve Problems: Both Addends Unknown

Another Look! You can show the same number in different ways.

Ashley has 4 flowers. Some are red and some are white. How many of each color flower does Ashley have?

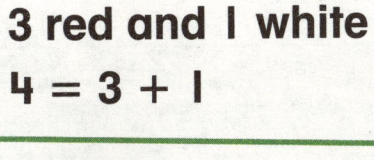

There are always 4 flowers!

3 red and 1 white
$4 = 3 + 1$

2 red and 2 white
$4 = 2 + 2$

1 red and 3 white
$4 = 1 + 3$

HOME ACTIVITY Give your child the following problem: "Dustin finds 8 leaves. Some are green. The rest are yellow. Write an addition equation to show the numbers of green and yellow leaves." Work with your child to choose parts of 8 and write an equation. Then repeat, choosing different parts of 8.

Draw a picture to show some frogs by the water and some in the grass. Then write an equation for each problem.

1. 9

$9 = \underline{} + \underline{}$

Topic 1 | Lesson 3

twenty-five 25

Draw a picture to show some frogs by the water and some in the grass. Then write an equation for the problem.

2. **Model** 8

   $8 = \underline{} + \underline{}$

   How does your equation show the parts?

3. **Higher Order Thinking** Laura picks 7 apples. Some apples are red and some are green. Fewer than 4 of the apples are red. How many of Laura's apples could be green? Explain how you know.

4. **Assessment** Mark sees 6 puppies. Some have spots and some do not.

   Match the number of puppies with spots with the number of puppies without spots that Mark could have seen.

1 with spots	4 without spots
2 with spots	2 without spots
4 with spots	5 without spots
5 with spots	1 without spots

Name _____

Lesson 1-4

Solve Problems: Take From

6 ducks swim in a pond. 2 ducks fly away. How can you use connecting cubes to show how many ducks are left? What subtraction equation can you write?

I can ...
solve word problems that involve taking from a group.

I can also model with math.

____ − ____ = ____

Topic 1 | Lesson 4   Digital Resources at SavvasRealize.com   twenty-seven **27**

7 ducks are in a pond. 3 ducks fly away. How many are still in the pond?

You can use cubes to model the problem.

7 is the whole.

3 is the part that you take from 7.

So, 4 is the **difference**.

You can **subtract** to solve the problem.

7 − 3 = 4

*7 **minus** 3 equals 4. There are 4 ducks still in the pond.*

Do You Understand?

Show Me! There are 6 bees in a yard. 2 bees fly away. How could you use connecting cubes to find the difference in this subtraction story?

☆ Guided Practice ☆

Complete the model. Then write a subtraction equation.

1. Dan has 6 pens. He gives 2 pens away. How many pens does Dan have left?

   6 − 2 = 4

2. 7 students play. 1 student leaves. How many students are still playing?

   ___ − ___ = ___

28 twenty-eight

Topic 1 | Lesson 4

Name _____

Independent Practice
Complete each model. Then write a subtraction equation.

3. 8 frogs sit on a log. 4 frogs jump away. How many frogs are still on the log?

8

____ − ____ = ____

4. 9 cats play. 6 cats run away. How many cats are still playing?

9

____ − ____ = ____

5. 7 bugs on a leaf. 2 bugs crawl away. How many bugs are still on the leaf?

7

____ − ____ = ____

6. Higher Order Thinking 8 students are in a reading group. Some of the students leave. How many students are still in the group? Do you have enough information to solve this problem? Explain.

Topic 1 | Lesson 4

Problem Solving Write an equation to match each problem. Use cubes or part-part-whole mats to solve.

7. Use Tools Lin has 9 stamps. She gives 4 stamps to Tom. How many stamps does Lin have now?

___ − ___ = ___

8. Use Tools Gloria has 8 flowers. She gives 5 flowers to her mother. How many flowers does Gloria have now?

___ − ___ = ___

9. Higher Order Thinking Find the missing number. Then write a subtraction story to match the equation.

7 − 2 = ___

10. Assessment 8 birds are in a tree. 6 birds fly away. How many birds are still in the tree?

Which subtraction equation matches the story?

Ⓐ 8 − 2 = 6   Ⓑ 8 − 7 = 1
Ⓒ 7 − 2 = 5   Ⓓ 8 − 6 = 2

Name _____

Homework & Practice 1-4
Solve Problems: Take From

Another Look! You can write a subtraction equation to match a number story.

6 cats are on a fence.
3 cats jump off. How many cats are still on the fence?

$6 - 3 = 3$

5 cats are on a fence.
2 cats jump off. How many cats are still on the fence?

$5 - 2 = 3$

HOME ACTIVITY Place 8 small objects, such as buttons, on the table. Take away several of the buttons. Ask your child to tell a subtraction story. Then have your child write a subtraction equation to match the story, such as $8 - 2 = 6$. Have your child count the buttons that are left to check if his or her answer is correct.

Write a subtraction equation to match each problem.

1. 9 apples are on a table. 7 apples roll off. How many apples are still on the table?

   ___ − ___ = ___

2. 10 crayons are in a box. 7 crayons fall out. How many crayons are still in the box?

   ___ − ___ = ___

Write a subtraction equation to match each number story.

3. **Reasoning** 6 bees are on a flower. 4 bees fly away. How many bees are still on the flower?

___ − ___ = ___

4. **Reasoning** 8 ducks are in the pond. 4 ducks get out. How many ducks are still in the pond?

___ − ___ = ___

5. **Higher Order Thinking** Find the missing number. Then write a subtraction story to match the equation.

$7 - 3 =$ ___

6. **Assessment** Jonah has 10 pebbles. He gives 2 pebbles to his sister.
How many pebbles does Jonah have now?

Which subtraction equation matches the story?

Ⓐ $9 - 4 = 5$
Ⓑ $10 - 3 = 7$
Ⓒ $8 - 1 = 7$
Ⓓ $10 - 2 = 8$

Name _____

Solve & Share

Lori sees 5 red cars and 3 blue cars. Did she see more red cars or blue cars? How many more? How can you tell?

Lesson 1-5
Solve Problems: Compare Situations

I can ...
solve word problems that involve comparing.

I can also use math tools correctly.

Topic 1 | Lesson 5

thirty-three 33

5 cats have blue hats.
2 cats have orange hats.
How many more blue hats are there than orange hats?

You can use cubes to compare.

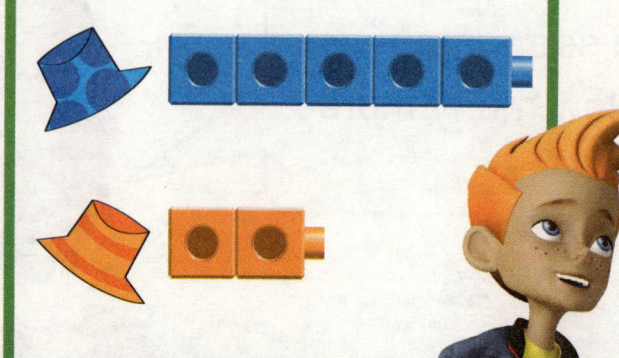

You can write a subtraction equation to compare.

$5 - 2 = 3$

There are 3 more blue hats than orange hats.

Do You Understand?

Show Me! If you have 2 groups of objects, how can you tell which group has more?

Guided Practice

Use cubes to write a subtraction equation. Then write how many more.

1. Peggy draws 6 frogs. Mike draws 3 frogs. How many more frogs does Peggy draw than Mike?

$\underline{6} - \underline{3} = \underline{3}$ _____ more frogs

Topic 1 | Lesson 5

Name _____

Independent Practice — Draw cubes to show the subtraction. Then write an equation to match the story. Tell how many.

2. Sue has 3 dogs. Julio has 1 dog. How many more dogs does Sue have?

___ − ___ = ___

___ more dogs

3. Tony counts 7 mice. He counts 5 more mice than Marie. How many mice does Marie count?

___ − ___ = ___

___ mice

Higher Order Thinking How many more blue birds than yellow birds? Use the picture to find the missing number for each problem.

4. ___ − 3 = 1

5. 6 − ___ = 1

Topic 1 | Lesson 5

thirty-five 35

Problem Solving Solve each problem below.

6. Number Sense 4 fish are in a tank. 2 fish are sold. How many fish are still in the tank? Write an equation to match the story. Then tell how many.

____ − ____ = ____

____ fish

7. Model Luis sees 5 green frogs. He sees 1 blue frog. How many more green frogs does Luis see than blue frogs? Write an equation to match the story. Tell how many more.

____ − ____ = ____

____ more green frogs

8. Higher Order Thinking Draw some yellow flowers. Draw more red flowers than yellow flowers. Write a subtraction equation that tells how many more red flowers than yellow flowers there are.

____ − ____ = ____

9. Assessment Bill counts 6 gray cats and 4 white cats.

How many more gray cats than white cats did Bill count?

Ⓐ 2
Ⓑ 4
Ⓒ 6
Ⓓ 10

You can draw a picture to help.

Name _____

Homework & Practice 1-5
Solve Problems: Compare Situations

Another Look! Match the red cubes with the blue cubes. Then count how many more.

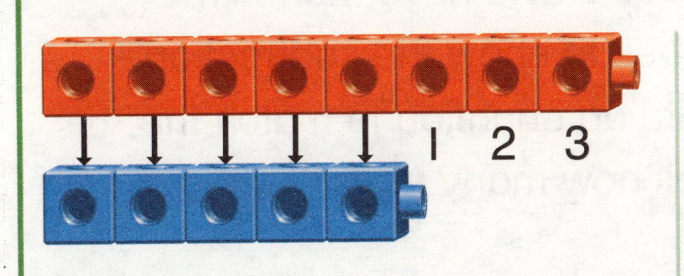

How many red cubes? 8
How many blue cubes? 5
How many more red cubes? 3

8 − 5 = 3

HOME ACTIVITY Give your child 5 blue buttons and 2 green buttons. Ask: Are there more blue or green buttons? Have your child tell how many more blue buttons than green buttons he or she has. Repeat with up to 10 blue buttons and 10 green buttons.

Write how many red cubes and blue cubes. Then tell how many more. Write a subtraction equation to match.

1. ___ red cubes
   ___ blue cubes
   Which color has more cubes? _____
   How many more? ___
   ___ − ___ = ___

2. ___ blue cubes
   ___ red cube
   Which color has more cubes? _____
   How many more? ___
   ___ − ___ = ___

Topic 1 | Lesson 5

Solve each problem below.

3. **Number Sense** Sam plays with 5 dogs. 3 dogs go home. How many dogs are still playing with Sam?

Write an equation to match the story. Then tell how many.

____ – ____ = ____

____ dogs

4. **Model** David has 6 tickets. Mimi has 2 tickets. How many more tickets does David have than Mimi? Draw cubes to show the subtraction. Then write an equation to match the story. Tell how many more.

____ – ____ = ____

____ more tickets

5. **Higher Order Thinking** Draw some red cubes. Draw more blue cubes than red cubes. Write a subtraction equation that shows how many more blue cubes than red cubes you drew.

____ – ____ = ____

6. **Assessment** Lucy has 6 apples. Julie has 7 apples. How many more apples does Julie have than Lucy?

0   1   6   7
Ⓐ   Ⓑ   Ⓒ   Ⓓ

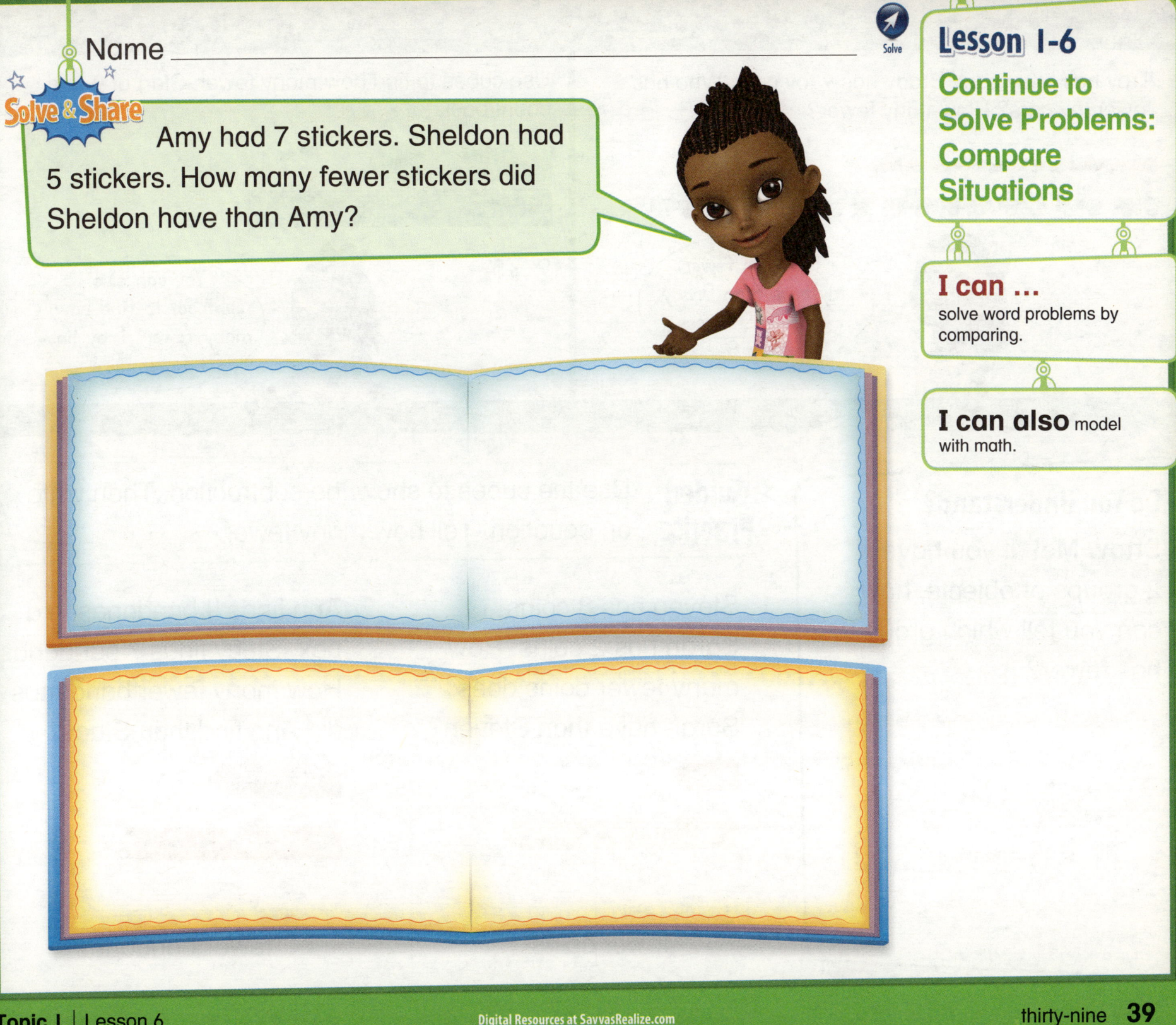

Name _____

Solve & Share

Amy had 7 stickers. Sheldon had 5 stickers. How many fewer stickers did Sheldon have than Amy?

Lesson 1-6
Continue to Solve Problems: Compare Situations

I can ...
solve word problems by comparing.

I can also model with math.

Topic 1 | Lesson 6

thirty-nine **39**

Troy has 5 toy cars. Brady has 9 toy cars. Who has fewer toy cars? How many fewer?

Troy has **fewer** toy cars than Brady because 5 is less than 9.

Use cubes to find how many fewer. Start at 9 and count back.

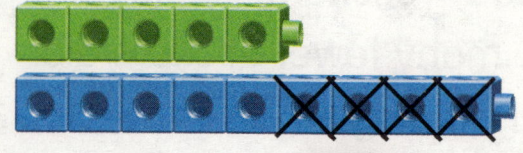

$9 - 5 = \underline{4}$

You can also subtract to find how many fewer. Troy has 4 fewer cars.

Do You Understand?

Show Me! If you have 2 groups of objects, how can you tell which group has fewer?

Guided Practice

Use the cubes to show the subtraction. Then write an equation. Tell how many fewer.

1. Steven has 8 coins. Sarah has 2 coins. How many fewer coins does Sarah have than Steven?

   ___ − ___ = ___

   ___ fewer coins

2. Ann finds 4 bandanas in a box. Stacy finds 7 bandanas. How many fewer bandanas did Ann find than Stacy?

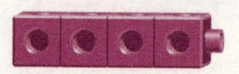

   ___ − ___ = ___

   ___ fewer bandanas

Name _____

Independent Practice
Use the pictures to show the subtraction. Then write an equation. Tell how many fewer.

3. Cheryl buys 10 apples at the store.
Kristina buys 5 apples at the store.
How many fewer apples did Kristina buy than Cheryl?

___ − ___ = ___

___ fewer apples

4. Beth writes on 3 cards.
Joseph writes on 9 cards.
How many fewer cards did Beth write on than Joseph?

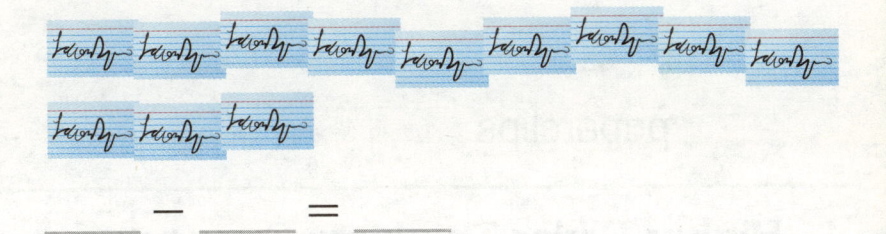

___ − ___ = ___

___ fewer cards

5. Higher Order Thinking Draw a picture to show the subtraction. Then write an equation. Tell how many fewer.

Keith makes 4 sandwiches.
Vince makes 8 sandwiches.
How many fewer sandwiches did Keith make than Vince?

___ − ___ = ___

___ fewer sandwiches

Topic 1 | Lesson 6

forty-one **41**

Problem Solving Solve the problems below.

6. Reasoning Leah uses 3 paperclips. Scott uses 6 paperclips. How many paperclips did Scott and Leah use in all? Write an equation. Then tell how many.

___ + ___ = ___

___ paperclips

7. Reasoning There are 7 oranges on a branch. 3 oranges fall off. How many oranges are still on the branch? Write a subtraction equation. Then tell how many.

___ − ___ = ___

___ oranges

8. Higher Order Thinking Draw some blue balloons. Draw fewer yellow balloons. Write an equation to match your drawing.

___ − ___ = ___

9. Assessment An orchard has 8 apple trees and 6 pear trees. Which of the following correctly answers how many more or fewer? Choose all that apply.

☐ 2 more pear trees
☐ 2 more apple trees
☐ 2 fewer pear trees
☐ 2 fewer apple trees

Name _____

Homework & Practice 1-6

Continue to Solve Problems: Compare Situations

Another Look! How many fewer orange cubes are there than purple cubes? Match the purple cubes with the orange cubes. Then count how many fewer. Write a subtraction equation to match.

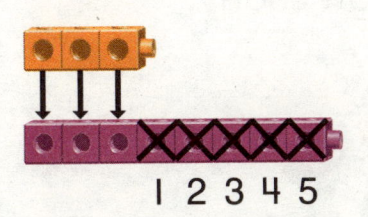

How many purple cubes? 8
How many orange cubes? 3
How many fewer orange cubes? 5

8 − 3 = 5

HOME ACTIVITY Give your child 3 buttons and 5 paperclips. Ask: Are there fewer buttons or paperclips? Have your child tell how many fewer buttons than paperclips he or she has. Your child may line them up to compare. Repeat with up to 10 buttons and 10 paperclips.

Write how many orange cubes and purple cubes. Then tell how many fewer. Write a subtraction equation to match.

1. 
____ purple cubes
____ orange cubes
Which color has fewer cubes? _____
How many fewer? ____
____ − ____ = ____

2. 
____ purple cubes
____ orange cubes
Which color has fewer cubes? _____
How many fewer? ____
____ − ____ = ____

Topic 1 | Lesson 6

forty-three 43

Solve the problems below.

3. Reasoning Hannah sells 5 muffins for a fundraiser. Then she sells 2 more. How many muffins does Hannah sell in all? Write an equation. Then tell how many.

___ + ___ = ___

___ muffins

4. Reasoning 6 butterflies are in a tree. 3 butterflies fly away. How many butterflies are left in the tree? Write an equation. Then tell how many.

___ − ___ = ___

___ butterflies

5. Higher Order Thinking Draw some red cubes. Draw fewer green cubes. Write an equation to match your drawing.

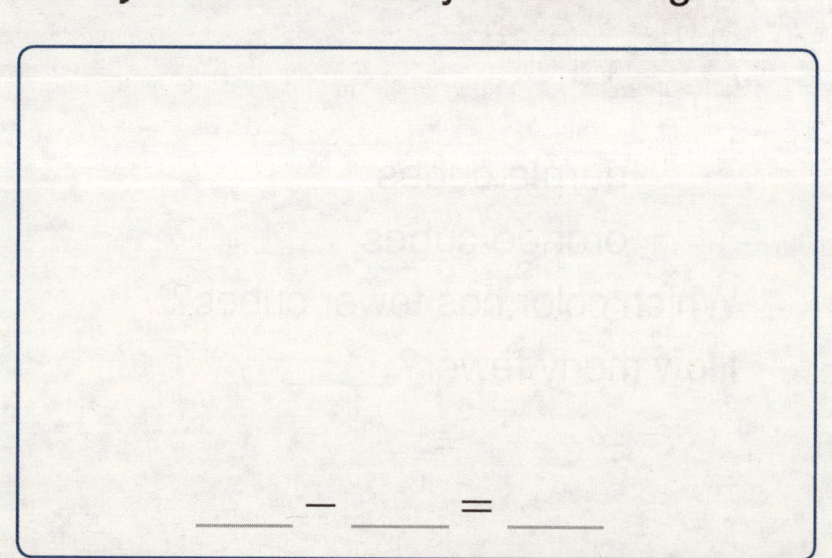

___ − ___ = ___

6. Assessment An animal shelter has 10 cats and 6 dogs. Which of the following correctly answers how many more or fewer? Choose all that apply.

☐ 4 more cats
☐ 4 more dogs
☐ 4 fewer cats
☐ 4 fewer dogs

Name _____

Solve & Share

5 train cars are on the track. Some more train cars join them. Now there are 9 train cars. How many train cars joined the first 5 train cars on the track? Use connecting cubes to model this story. Write an addition equation.

Lesson 1-7
Practice Solving Problems: Add to

I can ...
use addition or subtraction to help find a missing addend.

I can also model with math.

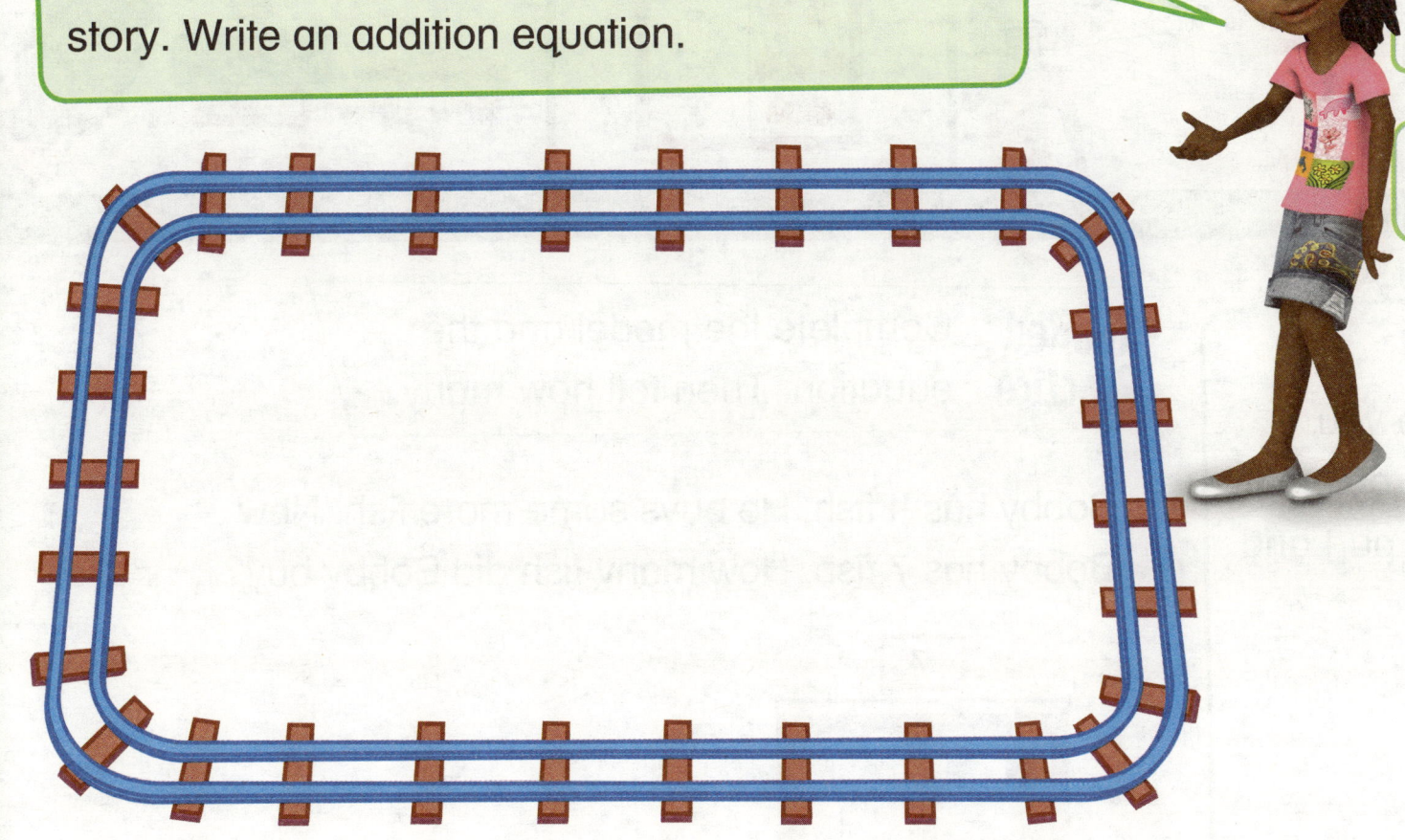

____ + ____ = ____

____ train cars joined.

A station has 7 train cars. Some more train cars roll into the station. Now there are 9 train cars. How many rolled in?

"7 plus what is 9?"

Use cubes and a model to help find the missing **addend**.

You can write an addition equation to match the story.

$$\underline{7} + \underline{2} = \underline{9}$$

addends   sum

"2 more train cars rolled in."

Do You Understand?

Show Me! How do you solve an addition problem if you know only one part and the sum?

Guided Practice

Complete the model and the equation. Then tell how many.

1. Bobby has 4 fish. He buys some more fish. Now Bobby has 7 fish. How many fish did Bobby buy?

   $4 + \underline{3} = 7$

   ____ fish

46 forty-six

Topic 1 | Lesson 7

Name _____

Independent Practice Complete the model. Then write an equation to match. Tell how many.

2. Mary has 4 stickers. Pat gives her some more stickers. Now Mary has 8 stickers. How many stickers did Pat give to Mary?

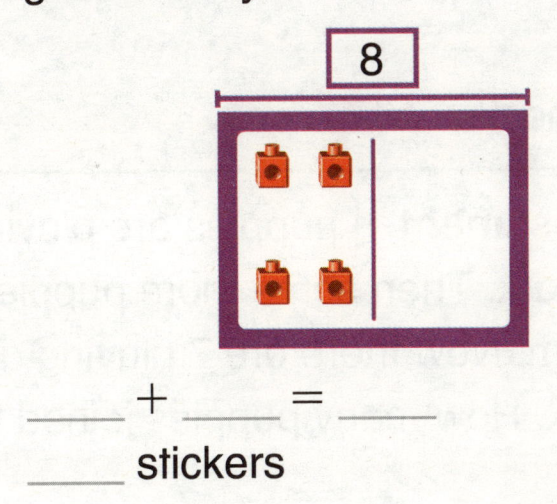

8

___ + ___ = ___
___ stickers

3. Billy reads 4 pages on Monday. He reads some more pages on Tuesday. He reads 10 pages in all. How many pages did Billy read on Tuesday?

10

___ + ___ = ___
___ pages

4. **Higher Order Thinking** Megan has 6 shoes in all. Some shoes are on the mat. 2 shoes are in the box. How many shoes are on the mat?

Draw a picture to solve. Then write an equation to match. Tell how many.

___ + ___ = ___
___ shoes on the mat

Topic 1 | Lesson 7

forty-seven **47**

Problem Solving Solve each problem.

5. Model Gabe's dog buries 4 bones on Monday. It buries some more bones on Friday. It buries 10 bones in all. How many bones did Gabe's dog bury on Friday? Write an equation to match the story. Then tell how many.

____ + ____ = ____

____ bones

6. Model Natalia has 3 pretzels and 7 crackers. How many snacks does she have in all? Write an equation to match the story. Then tell how many.

____ + ____ = ____

____ snacks

7. Higher Order Thinking 5 hamsters are in a cage. Some are brown and some are black. How many hamsters of each color could be in the cage? Draw a picture and write an equation to match the story.

____ = ____ + ____

8. Assessment 4 puppies are playing at the park. Then some more puppies join them. Now there are 7 playing at the park. How many puppies joined the first 4?

Which equation matches the story?

☐ $9 = 4 + 5$
☐ $7 = 6 + 1$
☐ $7 = 4 + 3$
☐ $10 = 7 + 3$

48 forty-eight

Topic 1 | Lesson 7

Name _____

Homework & Practice 1-7
Practice Solving Problems: Add to

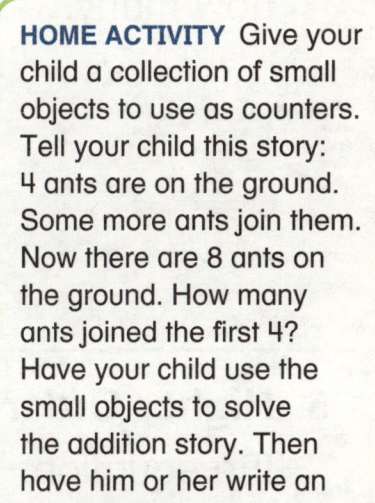

Another Look! You can use a model to solve an addition story and to write an equation.

Jim has 4 golf balls. He finds some more golf balls in his bag. Now Jim has 7. How many golf balls did Jim find in his bag?

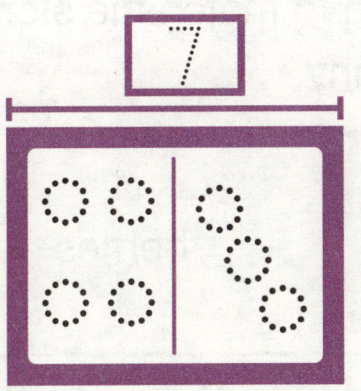

$4 + 3 = 7$

___ golf balls

HOME ACTIVITY Give your child a collection of small objects to use as counters. Tell your child this story: 4 ants are on the ground. Some more ants join them. Now there are 8 ants on the ground. How many ants joined the first 4? Have your child use the small objects to solve the addition story. Then have him or her write an equation to match.

Complete the model. Then write an equation to match. Tell how many.

1. 2 cats are playing. Some more cats come to play. Now there are 7 cats playing. How many cats came to play with the first 2 cats?

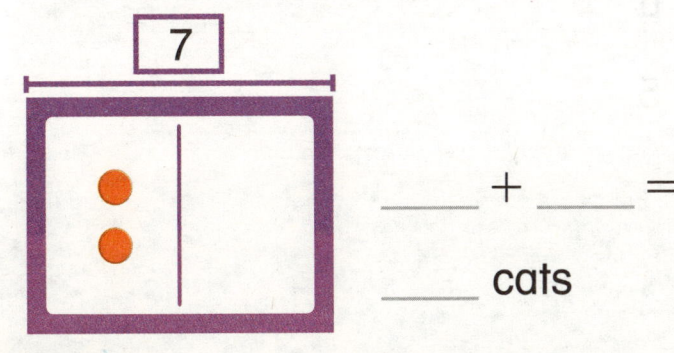

   ___ + ___ = ___

   ___ cats

2. 8 friends are eating lunch. Some more friends join them. Now there are 10 friends eating. How many more friends came to lunch?

   ___ + ___ = ___

   ___ friends

Topic 1 | Lesson 7 · Digital Resources at SavvasRealize.com · forty-nine **49**

Solve each problem.

3. Model Linda has 4 lemons. She buys 4 more lemons. How many lemons does Linda have now? Write an equation to match the story. Then tell how many.

___ + ___ = ___

___ lemons

4. Model Tia puts 5 berries in a basket. Brad adds some more berries to the basket. Now there are 9 berries in the basket. How many berries did Brad add? Write an equation to match the story. Then tell how many.

___ + ___ = ___

___ berries

5. Higher Order Thinking Complete the equation. Then write an addition story to match the equation.

8 + ___ = 10

6. Assessment Rashida has 7 coins. Gary gives her some more. Now Rashida has 10 coins. How many coins did Gary give Rashida?

Ⓐ 2
Ⓑ 3
Ⓒ 4
Ⓓ 5

Name _____

Solve & Share

Sophie sees 5 small pebbles by the lake. She also sees some big pebbles. She sees a total of 7 pebbles. How many big pebbles did Sophie see? Show how you know.

Lesson 1-8

Solve Problems: Put Together/ Take Apart

I can ...
solve word problems that involve putting together or taking apart.

I can also use math tools correctly.

Topic 1 | Lesson 8 | Digital Resources at SavvasRealize.com | fifty-one **51**

8 cats and dogs are on the dance floor. 5 dogs are dancing. How many cats are dancing?

Think about the whole and the part you know from the story.

8

?

There are 5 dogs dancing.

Subtract to find the missing part.

8

$8 - 5 = \underline{3}$

You can also add to find the missing part.

$5 + \underline{3} = 8$

6 7 8

3 cats are dancing.

Do You Understand?

Show Me! If you know the whole and one of the parts, how can you find the missing part?

☆ **Guided Practice** ☆ Complete the model. Then write an addition or subtraction equation.

1. Nick and Roger have 9 robots in all. Nick has 3 robots. How many robots does Roger have?

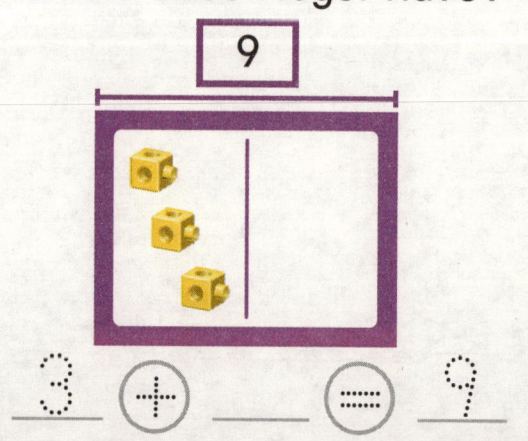

9

$\underline{3} \;\underline{(+)}\; \underline{} \;\underline{(-)}\; \underline{9}$

2. Gail has 6 kites. Some are red and some are blue. If 2 kites are red, how many kites are blue?

6

$\underline{} \;\bigcirc\; \underline{} \;\bigcirc\; \underline{}$

Topic 1 | Lesson 8

Name _____

Independent Practice — Complete the model. Then write an equation. Tell how many.

3. Jill walks 9 blocks. She walks 5 of the blocks with a friend. How many blocks did Jill walk by herself?

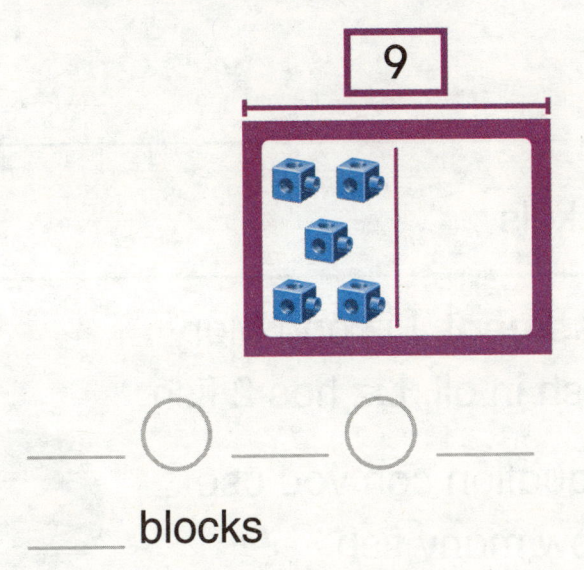

[9]

___ ◯ ___ ◯ ___

___ blocks

4. Rita has 3 yellow balloons. The rest of her balloons are pink. She has 7 balloons in all. How many pink balloons does Rita have?

[7]

___ ◯ ___ ◯ ___

___ pink balloons

5. **Higher Order Thinking** Henry has 8 shells in all. 3 shells are big. The rest are small. How many small shells does Henry have?

Draw a picture to solve. Then write an equation. Tell how many.

___ ◯ ___ ◯ ___

___ small shells

Topic 1 | Lesson 8

Problem Solving
Solve each problem. Draw a picture to help.

6. **Make Sense** Joe buys 2 red fish and some blue fish. He buys 9 fish in all. How many blue fish did Joe buy?

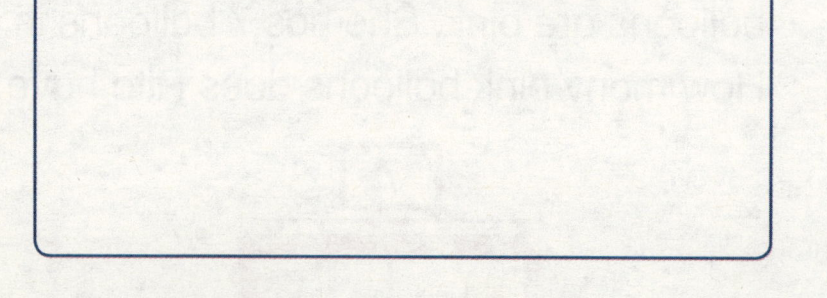

_____ blue fish

7. **Make Sense** Rachel has 8 nickels. She gives 4 nickels away. How many nickels does Rachel have left?

_____ nickels

8. **Higher Order Thinking** Nina has 8 stuffed animals. Some are bears and some are tigers. Draw a picture to show how many of each animal Nina could have. Then write the numbers.

_____ bears and _____ tigers

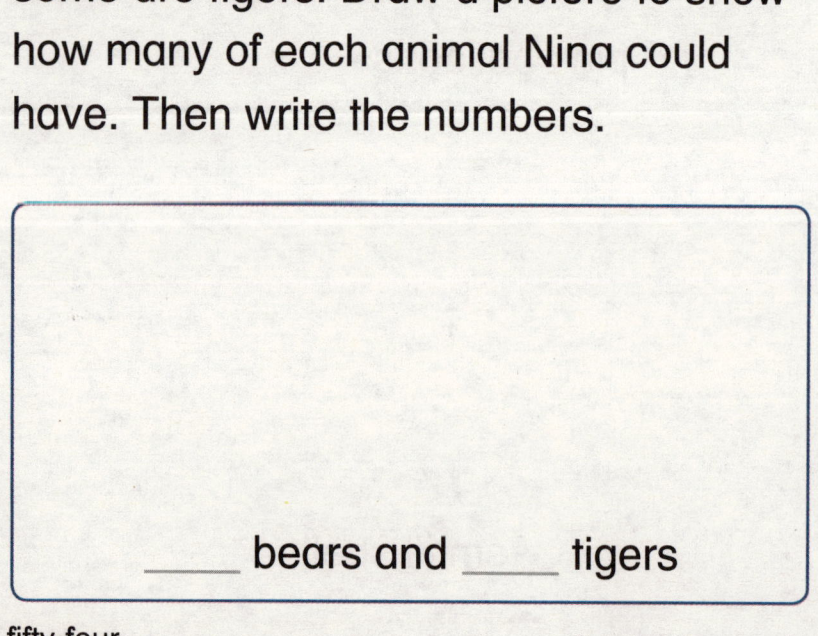

9. **Assessment** Liz and Mary have 7 fish in all. Liz has 2 fish. Which equation can you use to find how many fish Mary has?

Ⓐ $9 - 2 = 7$
Ⓑ $6 - 1 = 5$
Ⓒ $7 - 2 = 5$
Ⓓ $8 - 7 = 1$

The equation should match the number story.

Homework & Practice 1-8
Solve Problems: Put Together/Take Apart

Another Look! The dog has 8 spots on its back. 6 spots are brown. The rest are black. How many spots are black?

There are 8 spots in all. Subtract or count on from 6 to find the number of black spots.

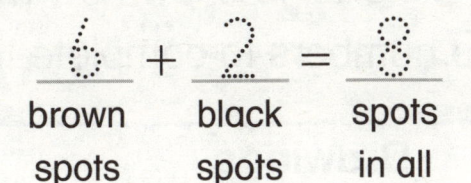

$\underline{8} - \underline{6} = \underline{2}$
spots in all — brown spots — black spots

$\underline{6} + \underline{2} = \underline{8}$
brown spots — black spots — spots in all

HOME ACTIVITY Place 6 to 9 small objects in a paper cup. Have your child pour some of the objects onto the table. Ask, "How many are still in the cup?" Have your child subtract the number of objects on the table from the number he or she started with. Then have your child count the objects that are left to check if his or her answer is correct.

Each dog has black and brown spots. Draw the missing brown spots. Write an equation to model the problem.

1. 6 spots in all

   ◯ ___ ◯ ___

2. 9 spots in all

   ◯ ___ ◯ ___

3. 7 spots in all

   ◯ ___ ◯ ___

Topic 1 | Lesson 8

Solve each problem below.

4. **Model** Juan has 9 shirts. 6 of his shirts are white. The rest are **NOT** white.

   Draw a picture and write an equation to show how many of Juan's shirts are **NOT** white.

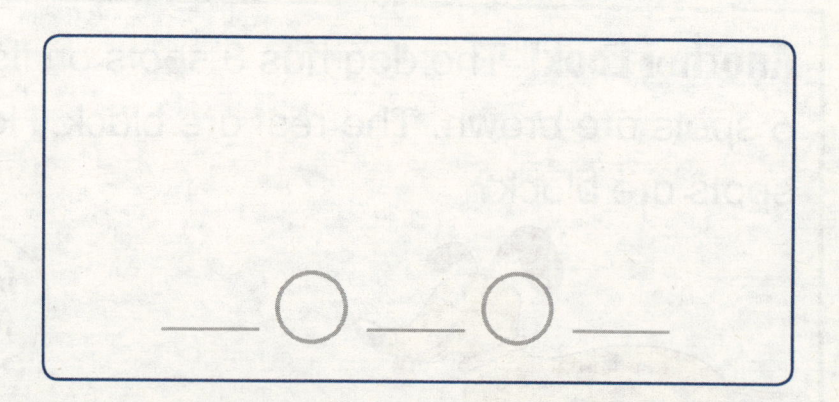

   ___ ◯ ___ ◯ ___

5. **Higher Order Thinking** Draw pictures to show how many there are of each fruit. Then write the numbers to complete the chart.

	Drawings	Bananas	Oranges
Amy has 8 in all.		4	
Joe has 6 in all.			2

6. **Assessment** Pedro and Deb have 9 baseball cards in all. Deb has 1 baseball card. How many baseball cards does Pedro have?

   Which equation matches the story?

   Ⓐ 9 − 1 = 8   Ⓑ 8 − 1 = 7   Ⓒ 8 − 7 = 1   Ⓓ 7 − 1 = 6

Name _____

Solve & Share

Mia needs 8 movie tickets. She has 5 movie tickets. She buys 3 more. Does she have enough tickets now? Explain how you know with pictures, numbers, or words.

Problem Solving

Lesson 1-9
Construct Arguments

I can ...
construct math arguments using addition and subtraction.

I can also add and subtract to 10.

Thinking Habits
How can I use math to explain my work?

Is my explanation clear?

Topic 1 | Lesson 9 | fifty-seven **57**

Does 6 − 2 have the same value as 1 + 3?

Make a math argument using pictures, numbers, or words to explain.

How can I use math to show my thinking?

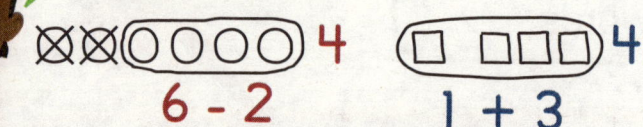

I can use pictures and numbers to make an argument.

⊗⊗◯◯◯◯ 4
6 − 2

☐ ☐☐☐ 4
1 + 3

I can use words and numbers to make an argument.

6 − 2 equals 4 and 1 + 3 equals 4.

6 − 2 equals 1 + 3. So, they have the same value.

Do You Understand?

Show Me! How are the two different math arguments alike and different?

Guided Practice Use pictures, numbers, or words to make an argument.

1. Marlen draws 6 tiles. 4 are red and the rest are green. How many green tiles did Marlen draw? Explain how you know.

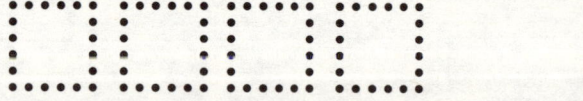

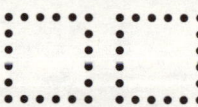

☐☐☐☐   ☐☐

Name _____

Independent Practice
Use pictures, numbers, or words to make an argument.

2. Jan has 7 pennies. She wants to buy a toy car for 3 pennies and a toy plane for 5 pennies. How many more pennies does Jan need? Explain.

3. Lidia has 7 pencils. Jon has 2 pencils. Who has fewer pencils? How many fewer? Explain.

4. **Higher Order Thinking** Max has 3 apples. He buys 2 more apples. He wants to keep 1 apple for himself and give 1 apple to each of his 5 friends.

Will Max have enough apples? Explain.

Topic 1 | Lesson 9

Problem Solving

✓ Performance Assessment

Lemonade Stand Alex opens a lemonade stand.

The table shows how many cups he sold on certain days. Use this information to solve the problems below.

Cups Sold

Friday	Saturday	Sunday	Monday
3	5	2	

5. **Explain** How many fewer cups did Alex sell on Friday than on Saturday? Use pictures, words, or numbers to make an argument.

6. **Make Sense** On Monday, Alex sells 4 more cups than he sold on Sunday. How many cups did Alex sell on Monday? Fill in the table. Explain how you know you are right.

Name _____

Homework & Practice 1-9
Construct Arguments

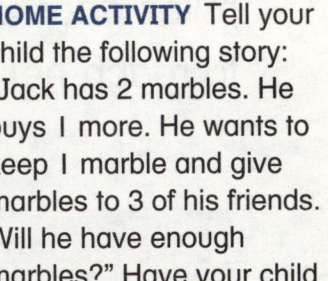

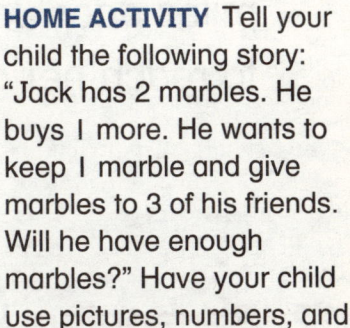

Another Look! Bill has 3 bananas. He buys 3 more. He wants to keep 1 banana for himself and give bananas to 5 of his friends.
Will Bill have enough bananas?
Explain.

The picture and equations show that Bill will have enough bananas.

3 + 3 = __6__ bananas    1 + 5 = __6__ people

HOME ACTIVITY Tell your child the following story: "Jack has 2 marbles. He buys 1 more. He wants to keep 1 marble and give marbles to 3 of his friends. Will he have enough marbles?" Have your child use pictures, numbers, and his or her own words to explain whether or not Jack has enough marbles.

Use pictures, numbers, or words to make an argument.

1. Tim has 7 toy cars. He buys 2 more. He wants to keep 1 toy car for himself and give 1 to each of his 8 friends. Will Tim have enough toy cars? Explain.

Topic 1 | Lesson 9

Performance Assessment

Walking Weekend Jada plans to walk a total of 8 miles in three days.

The table shows how many miles Jada walked on Friday and Saturday. How many miles does Jada need to walk on Sunday to reach her goal?

Miles Walked		
Friday	Saturday	Sunday
3	2	

2. **Reasoning** What do the numbers in the table mean? How can they help you solve the problem?

_____
_____
_____
_____

3. **Explain** How many miles does Jada need to walk on Sunday to reach her goal? Complete the table above. Explain how you found your answer. Use pictures, words, or numbers for your argument.

Name _____

Show the Word

Color these sums and differences. Leave the rest white.

| 4 | 3 | 5 |

TOPIC 1 — Fluency Practice Activity

I can ...
add and subtract within 5.

8 – 3	0 + 1	0 + 5	5 – 2	3 + 0	5 – 2	5 – 1	2 + 2	3 + 1
2 + 3	0 + 2	7 – 2	1 + 2	0 + 2	4 – 1	1 – 1	4 – 0	5 – 5
10 – 5	5 + 0	3 + 2	3 + 0	5 – 2	3 – 0	0 + 1	1 + 3	5 – 4
4 + 1	5 – 4	5 – 0	4 – 1	4 – 4	2 + 1	2 + 0	4 + 0	0 + 1
9 – 4	1 + 1	1 + 4	3 – 0	4 – 3	0 + 3	3 – 2	0 + 4	3 – 1

The word is

_____ _____ _____

Topic 1 | Fluency Practice Activity

sixty-three **63**

TOPIC 1 Vocabulary Review

Word List
- add
- addend
- difference
- equal
- equations
- fewer
- minus
- more
- part
- plus
- subtract
- sum
- whole

Understand Vocabulary

1. Write an addition equation.

   ___○___○___

2. Write a subtraction equation.

   ___○___○___

3. Circle the difference.

   $8 - 2 = 6$

4. Circle one part.

   $5 + 3 = 8$

5. Circle the plus sign.

   $3 + 4 = 7$

Use Vocabulary in Writing

6. Tell how to find $8 - 4$. Use at least one term from the Word List.

Name _____

Set A

Reteaching

You can solve problems about adding to.

Cindy has 3 shells. She finds 1 more. How many shells does Cindy have in all?

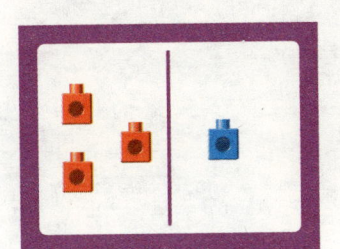

3 plus 1 more equals 4.

$3 + 1 = 4$

Write an addition equation to solve.

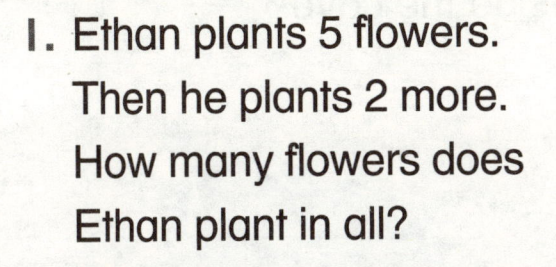

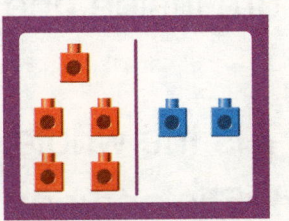

1. Ethan plants 5 flowers. Then he plants 2 more. How many flowers does Ethan plant in all?

___ + ___ = ___

Set B

You can solve problems about putting together.

Rick had 3 🟥 and 2 🟦. How many cubes does he have in all? The parts are 3 and 2.

$3 + 2$
$3 + 2 = 5$

Rick has 5 cubes in all.

Write the parts. Then write an addition equation to match the problem.

2. Brandon has 4 🟥 and 2 🟦. How many cubes does he have in all?

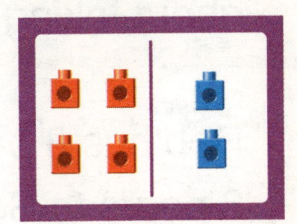

___ + ___

___ + ___ = ___

Topic 1 | Reteaching

sixty-five **65**

Set C

You can solve problems with both addends unknown.

There are 7 🐧 in all. How many are inside and outside the cave?

7 is the whole.
If 5 is one part,
2 is the other part.

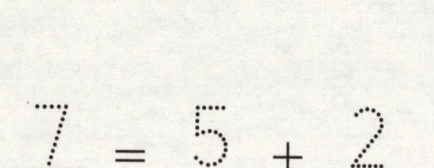

7 = 5 + 2

Draw a picture and write an equation to solve.

3. There are 6 🐧 in all. What is one way they could be inside and outside the cave?

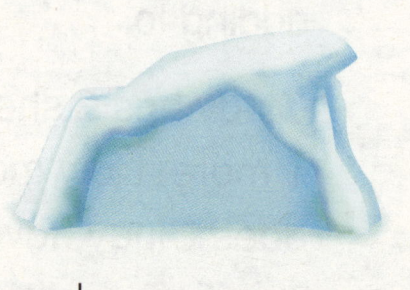

___ + ___ = ___

4. There are 9 🐧 in all. What is one way they could be inside and outside the cave?

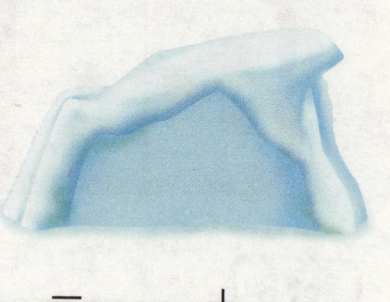

___ = ___ + ___

Set D

You can use cubes to model problems about taking from.

Rob has 8 pears. He gives 3 pears to Sal. How many pears does Rob have left?

8 − 3 = 5

Use cubes to help you complete the model. Then write an equation to match.

5. 7 carrots are in the garden. Karl picks 3 carrots. How many carrots are still in the garden?

___ − ___ = ___

Name _____

Set E

You can use cubes to solve problems about comparing.

Carla has 4 blue pencils. She has 3 yellow pencils. How many more blue pencils than yellow pencils does Carla have?

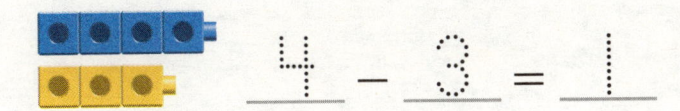

__4__ − __3__ = __1__

Write an equation to match each problem.

6. Mosi has 4 pens. Holly has 1 pen. How many more pens does Mosi have than Holly?

____ − ____ = ____

7. Martin has 7 baseballs and 3 soccer balls. How many more baseballs than soccer balls does he have?

____ − ____ = ____

Set F

You can use a model to solve problems about adding to.

Ty has 4 grapes. He takes some more grapes. Now he has 9 grapes. How many more grapes did Ty take?

9 = 4 + __5__

Ty took 5 more grapes.

Complete the model to solve the addition story.

8. Ivy has 2 fish in a bowl. She adds some more fish. Now Ivy has 5 fish in the bowl. How many fish did she add to the bowl?

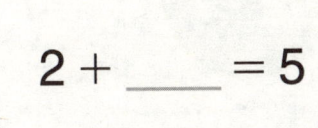

2 + ____ = 5

Set G

You can write an equation to find a missing part in a put together or take apart problem.

Tom has 9 shirts. Some are blue and some are red. If Tom has 4 red shirts, how many blue shirts does he have?

$9 - 4 = 5$

Complete the model. Then write an equation to solve.

9. John and Jenny have 8 pairs of shoes in all. Jenny has 4 pairs of shoes. How many pairs of shoes does John have?

___ ◯ ___ ◯ ___

Set H

Thinking Habits

Construct Arguments

How can I use math to explain my work?

Is my explanation clear?

Use pictures, numbers, or words to make an argument. Explain.

10. Luc has 4 goldfish and 2 guppies. He buys 2 more guppies. He wants to give 2 of each fish to a friend and keep 2 of each fish for himself. Explain whether Luc will have enough fish.

Name _____

1. There are 8 penguins. Some go inside the cave and some stay outside.

Match the number of penguins inside the cave with the number of penguins outside.

Inside: 5 penguins   4 penguins   7 penguins

Outside: 1 penguin   3 penguins   4 penguins

---

2. Sage had 8 peppers. She cooked 3 of them. How many peppers does Sage have left?

Write an equation that tells about the story.

____ − ____ = ____

3. Use the model to write the parts. Then write and solve an equation.

____ + ____

____ + ____ = ____

Topic 1 | Assessment

sixty-nine **69**

4. Trina has 4 markers. Her mother gives her 5 more markers.

Which addition equation shows how many markers Trina has in all?

Ⓐ 5 + 2 = 7
Ⓑ 4 + 3 = 7
Ⓒ 4 + 4 = 8
Ⓓ 4 + 5 = 9

5. George had 7 postcards. Then he gets some more. Now he has 9 postcards.

How many new postcards did George get?

Ⓐ 1
Ⓑ 2
Ⓒ 3
Ⓓ 4

6. Dante has 5 books. He wants to have 7 books in his collection. How many more books does Dante need to buy in order to have 7 in all?

7   5   4   2
Ⓐ   Ⓑ   Ⓒ   Ⓓ

Name _____

7. Lucy and Ellie have 6 cubes in all. Ellie has 5 cubes. How many cubes does Lucy have?

Which equations show the story? Choose all that apply.

$6 - 4 = 2$	$6 - 5 = 1$	$5 + 1 = 6$	$3 + 3 = 6$
☐	☐	☐	☐

8. Trina has 6 ribbons. Julie has 2 ribbons.
Which addition equation shows how many ribbons they have in all?

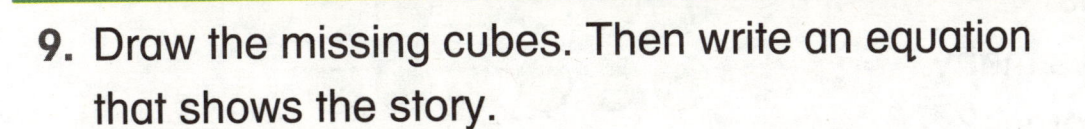

Ⓐ $7 = 5 + 2$
Ⓑ $8 = 5 + 3$
Ⓒ $8 = 6 + 2$
Ⓓ $9 = 6 + 3$

9. Draw the missing cubes. Then write an equation that shows the story.

Owen has 5 blocks. He gives 1 to Jordan. How many blocks does Owen have left?

____ $-$ ____ $=$ ____

Topic 1 | Assessment

seventy-one **71**

10. Hannah sees 7 flowers. Carrie sees 6 flowers. Which equation shows how many fewer flowers Carrie sees than Hannah?

$7 - 7 = 0$　　　$7 - 6 = 1$　　　$7 + 1 = 8$　　　$7 + 2 = 9$
　Ⓐ　　　　　　　Ⓑ　　　　　　　Ⓒ　　　　　　　Ⓓ

11. Laura has 4 pears. She buys 3 more pears. She wants to keep 2 pears for herself and give one to 6 of her friends.

    Use pictures and words to explain whether Laura will have enough pears.

12. Nikki has 8 tennis balls. Thomas has 6 tennis balls. Which equation shows many more tennis balls Nikki has than Thomas?

$4 + 4 = 8$　　　$8 - 3 = 5$　　　$2 - 0 = 2$　　　$8 - 6 = 2$
　Ⓐ　　　　　　　Ⓑ　　　　　　　Ⓒ　　　　　　　Ⓓ

Name _____

Skating Ribbons

Marta is an ice skater.
She wins ribbons for her skating.

TOPIC 1 — Performance Assessment

1. Marta wins 2 blue ribbons and 4 red ribbons.

   How many blue and red ribbons does she win in all?

   _____ ribbons

2. Marta has 4 red ribbons.
   She wins some more red ribbons.
   Now she has 7 red ribbons.

   How many more red ribbons did Marta win?

   _____ more

   Write an equation to show why your answer is correct.

Topic 1 | Performance Assessment

seventy-three 73

3. Marta has 8 yellow ribbons. What are 2 different ways she can place the ribbons on her door or her wall?

Write two different addition equations to show how she can put the ribbons on her door or her wall.

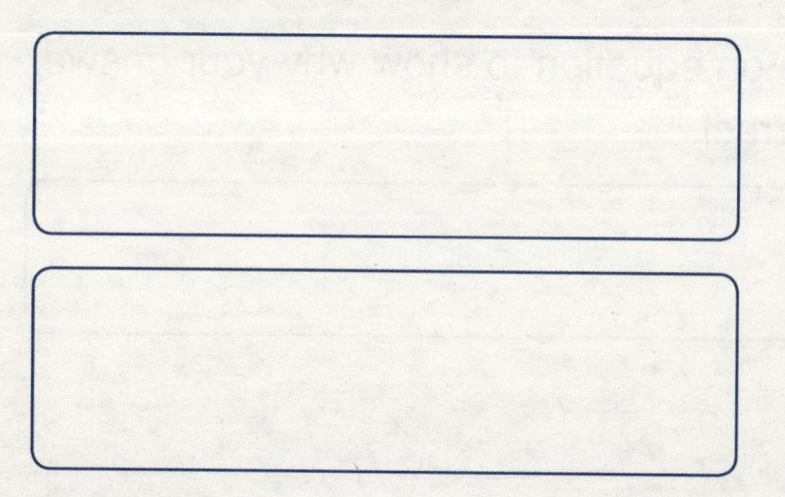

4. Marta has 8 yellow ribbons and 2 blue ribbons. How many more yellow ribbons than blue ribbons does Marta have?

____ more

5. Explain why your answer to Item 4 is correct. Use numbers, pictures, or words.

TOPIC 2: Fluently Add and Subtract Within 10

Essential Question: What strategies can you use while adding and subtracting?

The cap of an acorn protects it when it falls.

What could people wear to protect themselves from a fall?

Wow! Let's do this project and learn more.

Math and Science Project: Protect Yourself

Find Out Think of other things that help plants and animals survive. What helps humans survive? Do we make things to help protect us?

Journal: Make a Book Show what you found out. In your book, also:

- Make a list of some things that humans make to protect themselves.
- Make up and solve addition and subtraction problems about these things.

Name _____

Review What You Know

Vocabulary

1. Circle the numbers that are the **parts**.

   3 + 5 = 8

2. Circle the number that is the **whole**.

   3 + 5 = 8

3. Circle the symbol for **equals**.

   +   −   =

Understanding Addition

4. Write an addition sentence to match the picture.

   ___ + ___ = ___

5. Bob sees 5 bees. Ella sees some bees. They see 9 bees in all. How many bees did Ella see?

   Write an addition sentence to solve.

   ___ + ___ = ___

Making Numbers

6. Draw counters to show one way to make 8.

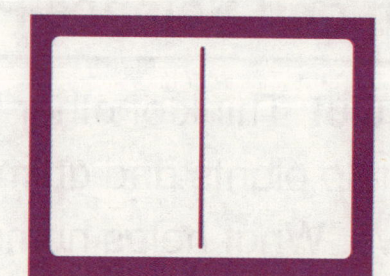

76 seventy-six

Topic 2

My Word Cards — Study the words on the front of the card. Complete the activity on the back.

number line

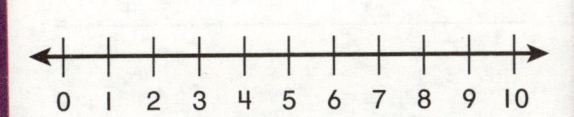

0 1 2 3 4 5 6 7 8 9 10

This **number line** shows the numbers 1 through 10.

doubles fact

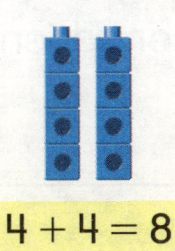

$4 + 4 = 8$

This is a **doubles fact**.

near doubles fact

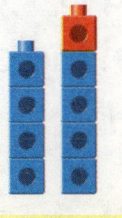

$4 + 5 = 9$

This is a **near doubles fact**.

Topic 2 | My Word Cards

My Word Cards

Use what you know to complete the sentences. Extend learning by writing your own sentence using each word.

An addition fact where one addend is 1 or 2 more than the other addend is a

_____

_____.

An addition fact where one addend is the same as the other addend is a

_____.

A _____

_____

shows numbers in order from left to right.

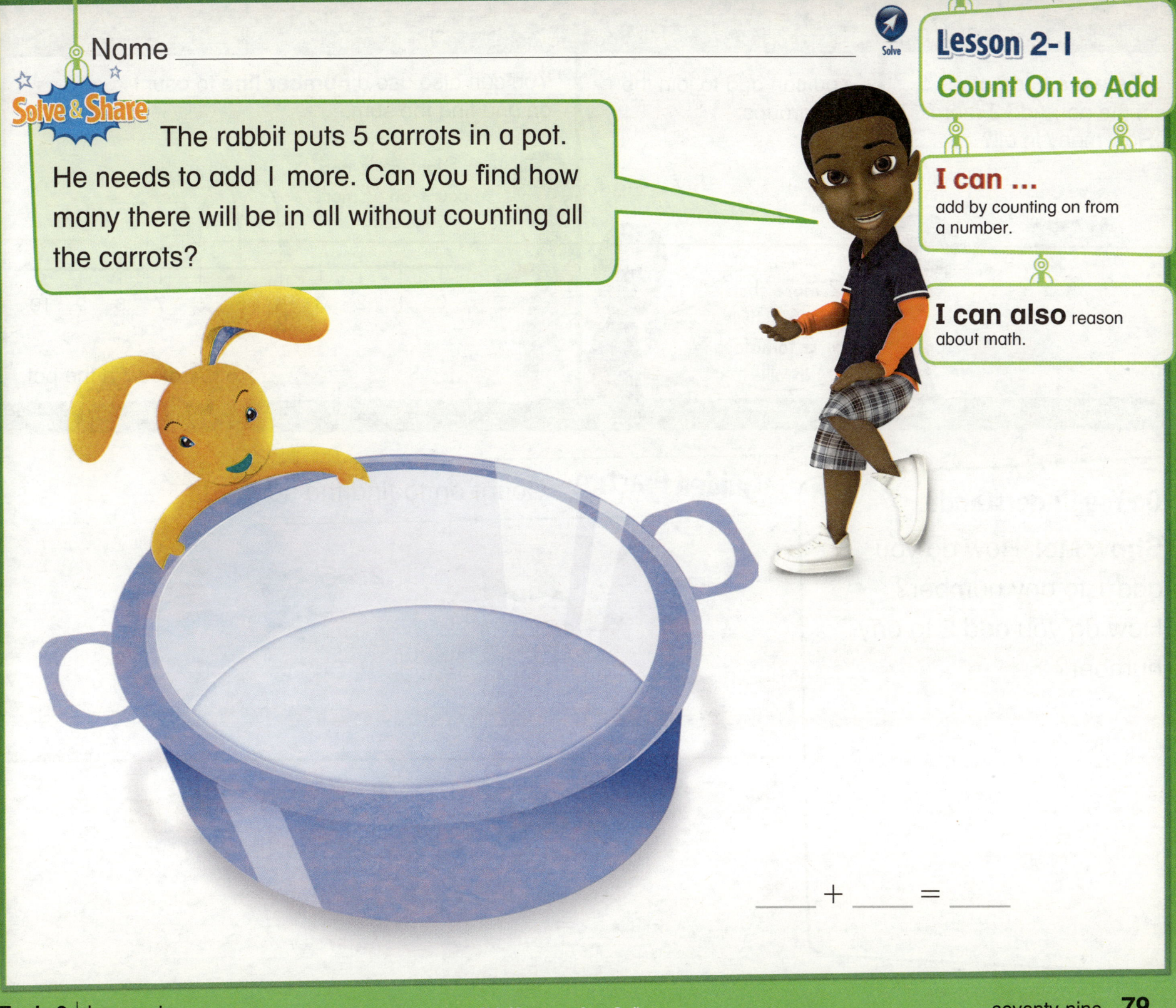

Name _____

Solve & Share

The rabbit puts 5 carrots in a pot. He needs to add 1 more. Can you find how many there will be in all without counting all the carrots?

Lesson 2-1
Count On to Add

I can ...
add by counting on from a number.

I can also reason about math.

____ + ____ = ____

Topic 2 | Lesson 1 seventy-nine **79**

There are 4 tomatoes in the pot. Add 2 more. How many in all?

You can add to join the two groups.

$4 + 2 = 6$

2 more than 4 is 6. There are 6 tomatoes in all!

You can also use a **number line** to count on and find the sum.

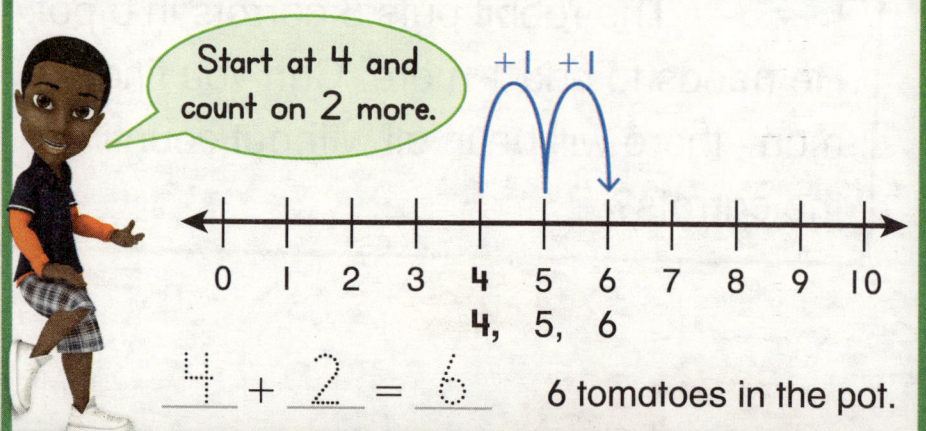

Start at 4 and count on 2 more.

4, 5, 6

$4 + 2 = 6$

6 tomatoes in the pot.

Do You Understand?

Show Me! How do you add 1 to any number? How do you add 2 to any number?

Guided Practice Count on to find the sum.

1.  $3 + 2 = 5$

2.  ___ + ___ = ___

3.  ___ + ___ = ___

4.  ___ + ___ = ___

Topic 2 | Lesson 1

Name _____

Independent Practice
Count on to add. Use the number line to help.

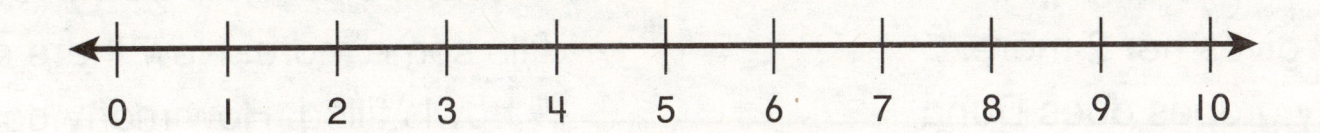

`<----+----+----+----+----+----+----+----+----+----+---->`
 0   1   2   3   4   5   6   7   8   9   10

5. $3 + 2 =$ ___

6. $8 + 1 =$ ___

7. $7 + 1 =$ ___

8. $9 + 1 =$ ___

9. $4 + 3 =$ ___

10. $9 = 6 +$ ___

11. $2 + 6 =$ ___

12. $6 = 5 +$ ___

13. $5 + 3 =$ ___

14. **Number Sense** Circle **True** or **False**. Count on to help you.

$8 + 0 = 8$ True   False $3 + 1 = 5$ True   False

$7 + 1 = 7$ True   False $6 = 4 + 0$ True   False

$8 = 6 + 2$ True   False $5 + 2 = 7$ True   False

Topic 2 | Lesson 1

Problem Solving Draw a picture and write an equation to solve each problem. Decide how many you need to count on to solve.

15. **Model** Dana has 8 grapes. Her sister gives her 2 more. How many grapes does Dana have now?

___ + ___ = ___

Dana has ___ grapes.

16. **Model** Anna fills 6 bowls. Jason fills some more. Now there are 9 bowls filled. How many bowls did Jason fill?

___ + ___ = ___

Jason filled ___ bowls.

17. **Higher Order Thinking** Max has 1 more carrot than Jena. Jena has 3 more carrots than Sal. Sal has 4 carrots.

Write how many carrots each person has.

___   ___   ___
Max   Jena   Sal

18. **Assessment** Maria is 2 years older than Tim. She is 7 years old.

Which addition equation helps you find Tim's age?

Ⓐ $2 + 7 = 9$

Ⓑ $5 + 1 = 6$

Ⓒ $5 - 2 = 3$

Ⓓ $5 + 2 = 7$

Name _____

Homework & Practice 2-1
Count On to Add

Another Look! Count on to find the sum.

Add 1 and the sum is 1 more.

3, 4

3 + 1 = 4

Add 2 and the sum is 2 more.

3, 4, 5

3 + 2 = 5

Add 3 and the sum is 3 more.

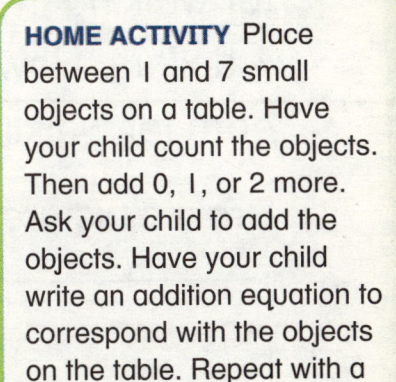

3, 4, 5, 6

3 + 3 = 6

HOME ACTIVITY Place between 1 and 7 small objects on a table. Have your child count the objects. Then add 0, 1, or 2 more. Ask your child to add the objects. Have your child write an addition equation to correspond with the objects on the table. Repeat with a different number of objects.

Count on to complete the addition facts.

1.  6, ___

   6 + 1 = ___

2.  5, ___, ___, ___

   5 + 3 = ___

3.  7, ___, ___

   7 + 2 = ___

Topic 2 | Lesson 1

eighty-three 83

Count on to solve each problem below.

4. Max earns 5 dollars for washing dishes. Then he earns some more dollars for walking the dog. In all, Max earns 7 dollars. How many dollars did Max earn for walking the dog?

Draw a picture. Write the number.

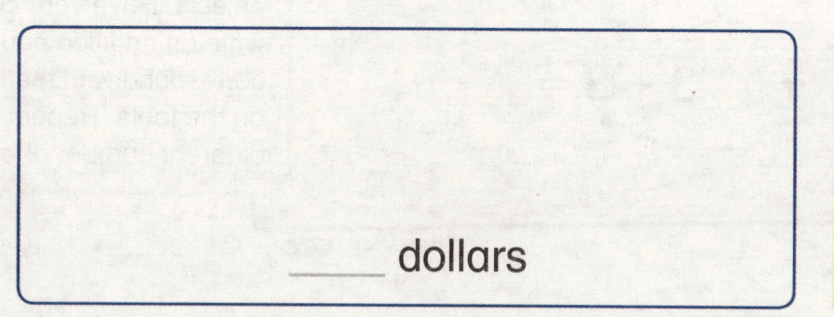

_____ dollars

5. Emma reads 7 books in one week. Then she reads 3 more books. How many books did Emma read in all?

Draw a picture. Write the number.

_____ books

6. Higher Order Thinking Write the missing number.

$3 + 2 = 2 + $ _____

Use the picture to help!

7. Assessment There are 6 bees in a hive. 3 more bees fly in. Count on to find how many bees are in the hive now.

Which addition fact matches the story?

Ⓐ $6 + 2 = 8$

Ⓑ $6 + 3 = 9$

Ⓒ $6 + 0 = 6$

Ⓓ $8 + 0 = 8$

84 eighty-four

Topic 2 | Lesson 1

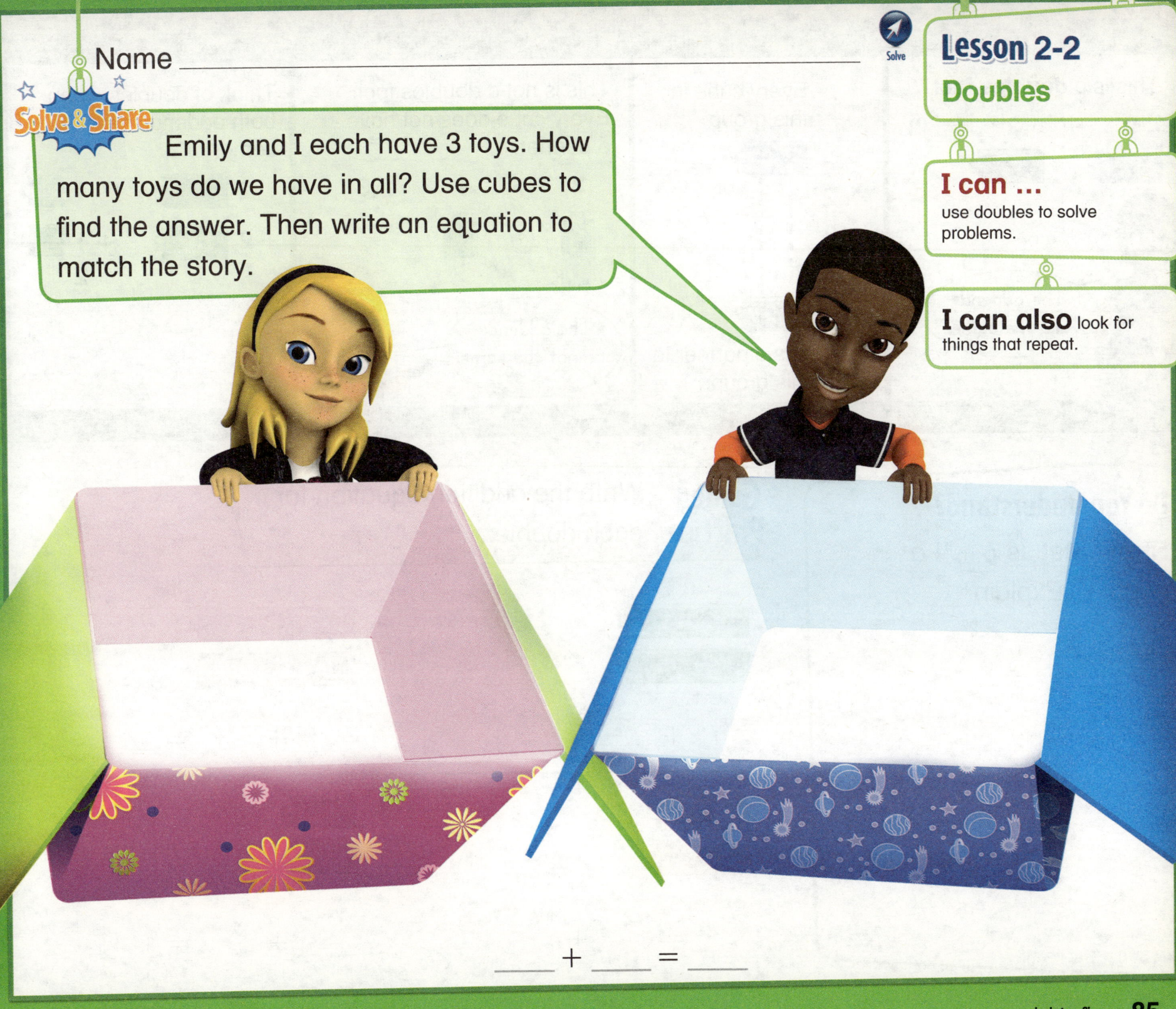

Name _____

Solve & Share

"Emily and I each have 3 toys. How many toys do we have in all? Use cubes to find the answer. Then write an equation to match the story."

Lesson 2-2
Doubles

I can ...
use doubles to solve problems.

I can also look for things that repeat.

___ + ___ = ___

Topic 2 | Lesson 2

This is a **doubles fact**.

2 + 2 = 4

The addends are the same.

Every cube in this group

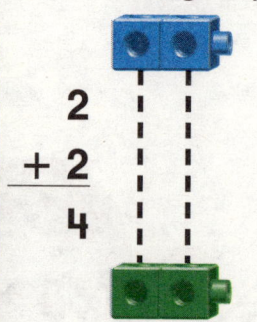

2
+ 2

4

has a partner in this group.

This is not a doubles fact. Every cube does not have a partner.

2 + 1 = 3

The addends are not the same.

Think of doubles when both addends are the same.

2
+ 2

4

1
+ 1

2

Do You Understand?

Show Me! Is 6 + 4 a double? Explain.

Guided Practice

Write the addition equation for each double.

1. 4 + 4 = 8

2. ___ + ___ = ___

3. ___ = ___ + ___

4. ___ + ___ = ___

Name _____

Independent Practice Write the sum for each doubles fact.

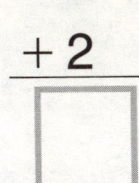

5. ___ + ___ = ___

6. ___ + ___ = ___

7. ___ + ___ = ___

8. 2
   +2
   ☐

9. 4
   +4
   ☐

10. 0
    +0
    ☐

11. **Vocabulary** Draw a picture to show a **doubles fact**. Write the addition equation to match your drawing.

___ + ___ = ___

Topic 2 | Lesson 2

eighty-seven **87**

Problem Solving
Draw a picture to solve each problem.

12. Make Sense Neela makes 4 pies. John makes the same number of pies.

How many pies do Neela and John make in all?

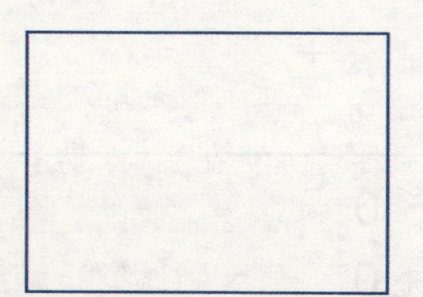

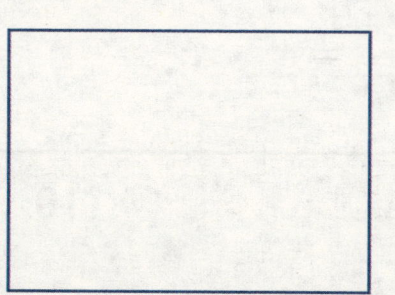

_____ pies

13. Make Sense Kim has 2 pockets. She has 5 pennies in each pocket.

How many pennies does Kim have in all?

_____ pennies

14. Higher Order Thinking Is there a doubles fact that has a sum of 9? Draw a picture to find out. Circle **Yes** or **No**.

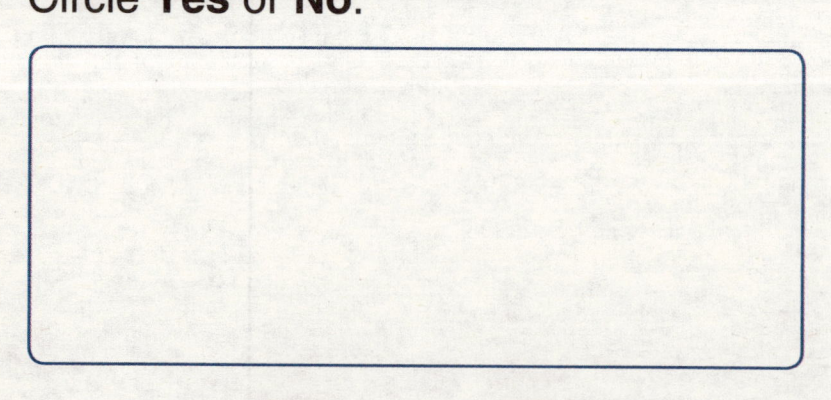

Yes   No

15. Assessment Danny has 2 baskets. He has the same number of pencils in each basket. He has 6 pencils in all.

How many pencils does Danny have in each basket?

3　　4　　5　　6
Ⓐ　　Ⓑ　　Ⓒ　　Ⓓ

Name _____

Homework & Practice 2-2
Doubles

Another Look! When the addends are the same, it is a doubles fact. Here are some doubles facts.

$$2 + 2 = 4$$

$$\begin{array}{r}2\\+2\\\hline 4\end{array}$$

↑ addend ↑ addend ↑ sum

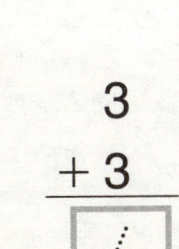

$$\begin{array}{r}3\\+3\\\hline \boxed{6}\end{array}$$

$$3 + 3 = 6$$

↑ addend ↑ addend ↑ sum

HOME ACTIVITY Have your child use small objects to show 2 groups of 4. Then ask your child to write an addition equation to show the double (4 + 4 = 8). Repeat for other doubles of 1 + 1 through 5 + 5.

Write the sum for each doubles fact.

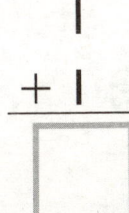

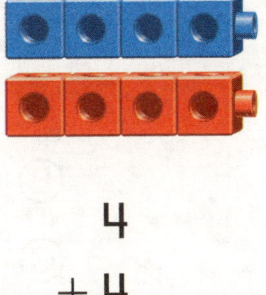

1. $\begin{array}{r}1\\+1\\\hline\ \end{array}$

2. $\begin{array}{r}4\\+4\\\hline\ \end{array}$

3. $\begin{array}{r}5\\+5\\\hline\ \end{array}$

Topic 2 | Lesson 2

eighty-nine 89

Write an addition equation to solve each problem.

4. Reasoning Owen paints 5 pictures. Luis paints 5 pictures, too. How many pictures did Owen and Luis paint in all?

____ + ____ = ____

5. Reasoning Tess and Maya grow 6 flowers in all. Tess grows 3 flowers. How many flowers does Maya grow?

____ = ____ + ____

Write the missing number for each problem.

6. Algebra

$4 = 2 + $ ____

7. Algebra

____ $+ 4 = 8$

8. Algebra

$0 + $ ____ $= 0$

9. Higher Order Thinking There are 6 marbles in all. How many marbles are inside the cup?

____ marbles are inside the cup.

10. Assessment There are 10 marbles in all. There are 5 marbles outside the cup. How many marbles are inside the cup?

Ⓐ 2
Ⓑ 4
Ⓒ 5
Ⓓ 10

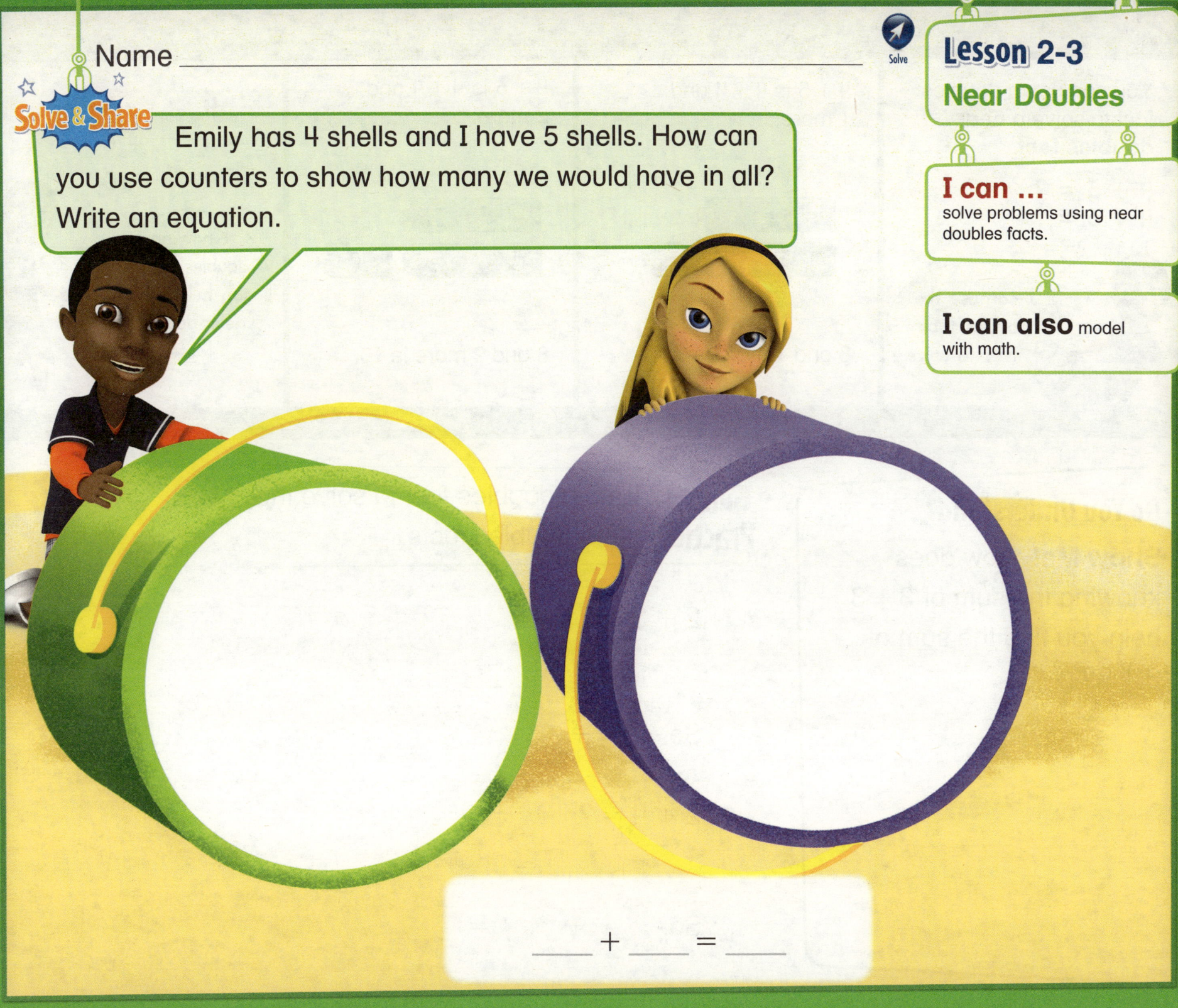

Name _____

Solve & Share

Emily has 4 shells and I have 5 shells. How can you use counters to show how many we would have in all? Write an equation.

Lesson 2-3
Near Doubles

I can ...
solve problems using near doubles facts.

I can also model with math.

___ + ___ = ___

Topic 2 | Lesson 3 ninety-one **91**

You can use a doubles fact to solve a **near doubles fact**.

$4 + 5 = ?$
$4 + 6 = ?$

I can use the doubles fact $4 + 4$ to solve.

$4 + 5$ is $4 + 4$ and 1 more.

8 and 1 more is 9.

$4 + 6$ is $4 + 4$ and 2 more.

8 and 2 more is 10.

$$\begin{array}{r} 4 \\ +5 \\ \hline 9 \end{array} \quad \begin{array}{r} 4 \\ +6 \\ \hline 10 \end{array}$$

Knowing doubles facts can help solve near doubles facts.

Do You Understand?

Show Me! How does knowing the sum of $3 + 3$ help you find the sum of $3 + 4$?

Guided Practice

Use a doubles fact to solve the near doubles facts.

1. $2 + 3 = ?$

   $\underline{2} + \underline{2} = \underline{4}$

   So, $\underline{2} + \underline{3} = \underline{5}$

2. $2 + 4 = ?$

   ___ + ___ = ___

   So, ___ + ___ = ___

Name _____

Independent Practice Use a doubles fact to solve the near doubles facts.

3. 3 + 4 = ?

___ + ___ = ___

So, ___ + ___ = ___

4. 3 + 5 = ?

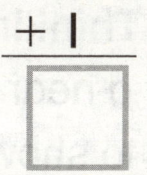

___ + ___ = ___

So, ___ + ___ = ___

5. 4
   +5
   ☐

6. 2
   +4
   ☐

7. 2
   +1
   ☐

8. 3 + 2 = ___

9. 1 + 3 = ___

Think of a doubles fact and add 1 or 2 more.

Number Sense Write the missing numbers.

10. If 2 + ___ = 4, then 2 + ___ = 5.

11. If 4 + ___ = 8, then 4 + ___ = 9.

Topic 2 | Lesson 3

ninety-three **93**

Problem Solving Use a doubles fact to solve each near doubles fact. Write an equation to match each problem.

12. **Reasoning** Omar eats 2 pears. Jane eats 2 pears and then 1 more. How many pears did Omar and Jane eat in all?

____ + ____ = ____

Omar and Jane eat ____ pears.

13. **Reasoning** Sam finds 3 shells and Jack finds 4 shells. How many shells did they find in all?

____ + ____ = ____

Sam and Jack find ____ shells.

14. **Higher Order Thinking** Write a story problem about a near double. Then draw a picture to show the story.

15. **Assessment** Patty plays 4 games of jump rope. Mary plays 4 games of jump rope and then 1 more. How many games of jump rope did Patty and Mary play in all?

Ⓐ 10
Ⓑ 9
Ⓒ 8
Ⓓ 7

You can use a near doubles fact to help solve the problem.

Homework & Practice 2-3
Near Doubles

Another Look! You can use doubles to add near doubles.

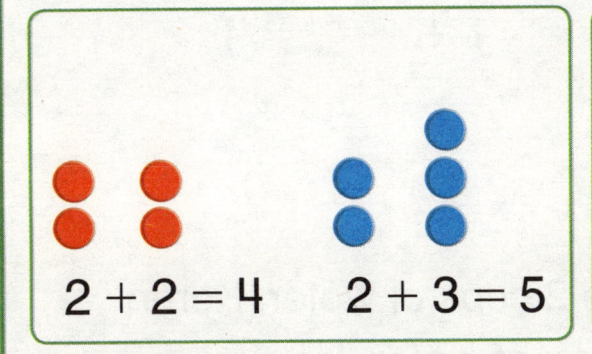

$2 + 2 = 4$ $2 + 3 = 5$

$3 + 3 = 6$ $3 + 4 = 7$

If $2 + 2 = 4$, then $2 + 3$ is 1 more.
$2 + 3 = 5$

If $3 + 3 = 6$, then $3 + 4$ is 1 more.
$3 + 4 = 7$

HOME ACTIVITY Play a game with small objects, like pennies. First, use the pennies to represent numbers that are doubles. Ask your child to add the set of doubles. Then add another penny and ask your child to add the set of near doubles.

Add the doubles. Then add the near doubles.

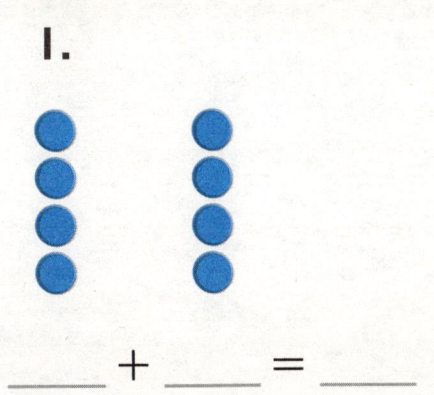

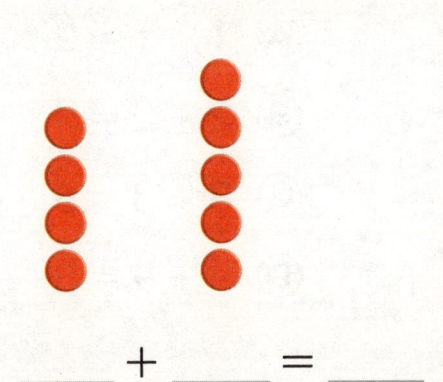

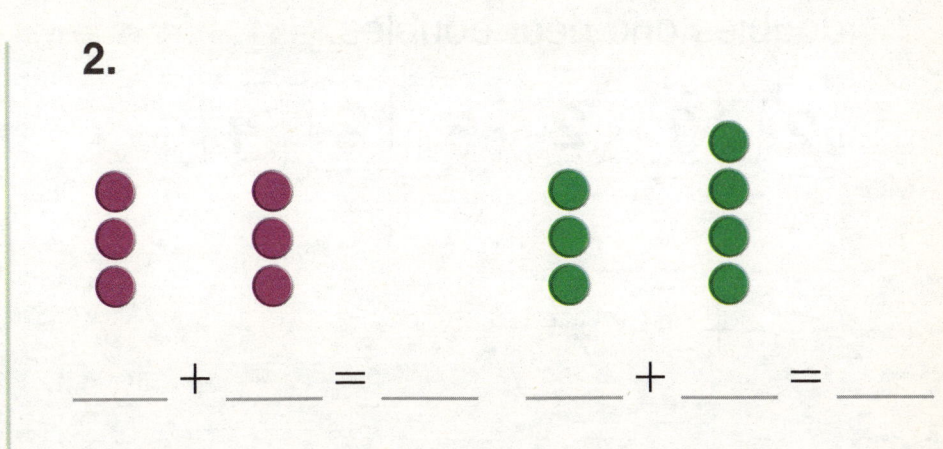

1. ___ + ___ = ___   ___ + ___ = ___

2. ___ + ___ = ___   ___ + ___ = ___

Topic 2 | Lesson 3

Find the number to complete each near doubles fact.

3. Algebra

3 + ___ = 7

4. Algebra

9 = 4 + ___

5. Algebra

1 + ___ = 4

Write an addition equation to solve each problem.

6. Sandy plays 3 games. Bill plays 3 games and then 1 more. How many games did Sandy and Bill play in all?

___ = ___ + ___

Sandy and Bill played ___ games.

7. Nina drinks 2 cups of water. Karen drinks 4 cups of water. How many cups did they drink in all?

___ + ___ = ___

Nina and Karen drank ___ cups.

8. **Higher Order Thinking** Use each card once to write addition equations using doubles and near doubles.

2   3   2   5   2   4

___ + ___ = ___

___ + ___ = ___

9. **Assessment** Which doubles fact can help you solve 4 + 5 = ?

Ⓐ 1 + 1 = 2

Ⓑ 2 + 2 = 4

Ⓒ 3 + 3 = 6

Ⓓ 4 + 4 = 8

Name _____

Solve & Share

Put some counters on the bottom row of the ten-frame. What addition equation can you write to match the counters?

Lesson 2-4
Facts with 5 on a Ten-Frame

I can ...
use a ten-frame to help solve addition facts with 5 and 10.

I can also model with math.

____ + ____ = ____

Topic 2 | Lesson 4

ninety-seven **97**

You can use a ten-frame to show an addition fact with 5.

$5 + 3 = ?$

Start with 5. Then add 3 more.

5 and 3 more is 8.

There are 8 counters in the ten-frame.

$5 + 3 = 8$

The ten-frame shows another addition fact. You have 8. Make 10.

2 boxes are empty. Add 2.

8 plus 2 more is 10.

$8 + 2 = 10$

Do You Understand?

Show Me! How does a ten-frame help you add $5 + 4$?

Guided Practice

Look at the ten-frames. Write an addition fact with 5. Then write an addition fact for 10.

1. $5 + \underline{2} = 7$
   $7 + \underline{3} = 10$

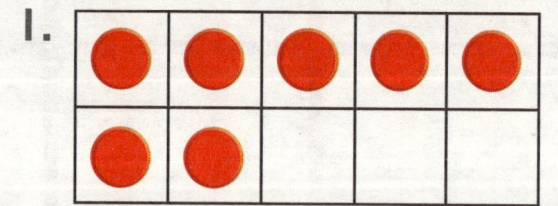

2. $5 + \underline{} = \underline{}$
   $\underline{} + \underline{} = 10$

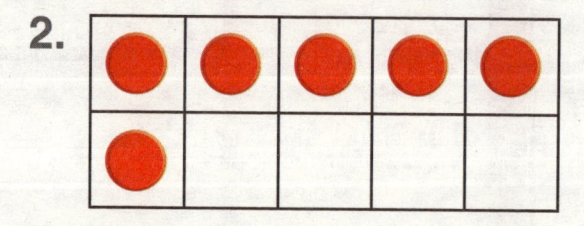

Independent Practice Look at the ten-frames. Write an addition fact with 5. Then write an addition fact for 10.

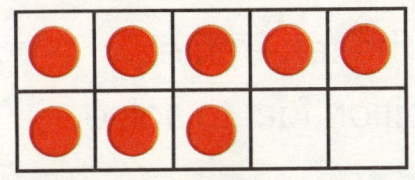

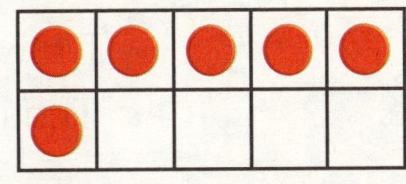

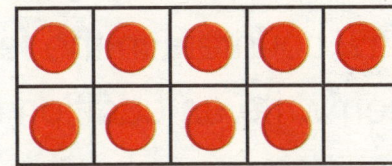

3.

5 + ___ = ___

___ + ___ = 10

4.

5 + ___ = ___

___ + ___ = 10

5.

5 + ___ = ___

___ + ___ = 10

6. **Higher Order Thinking** Using 2 colors, draw counters in the ten-frames to match the addition equations. Then write the missing numbers.

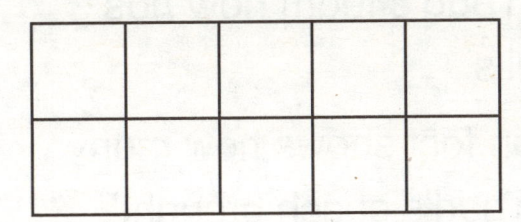

8 + ___ = 10

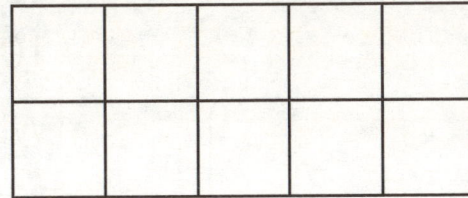

7 + ___ = 10

Which number will make 10?

Topic 2 | Lesson 4

ninety-nine **99**

Problem Solving Solve each problem below.

7. Model A team has 5 softballs. The coach brings 3 more. How many softballs does the team have now?

Draw counters in the ten-frame. Then write an addition fact to solve.

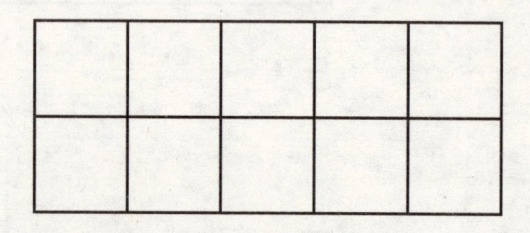

____ + ____ = ____   ____ softballs

8. Model Kami reads 5 books. Sue reads 4 books. How many books did the girls read in all?

Draw counters in the ten-frame. Then write an addition fact to solve.

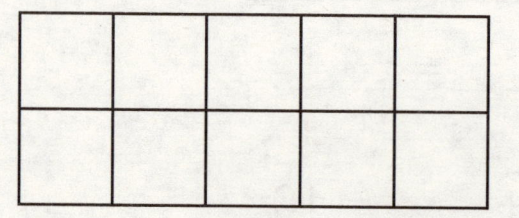

____ + ____ = ____   ____ books

9. Higher Order Thinking Write a new story about adding to 10 in the ten-frame in Item 7. Then write an equation for your story.

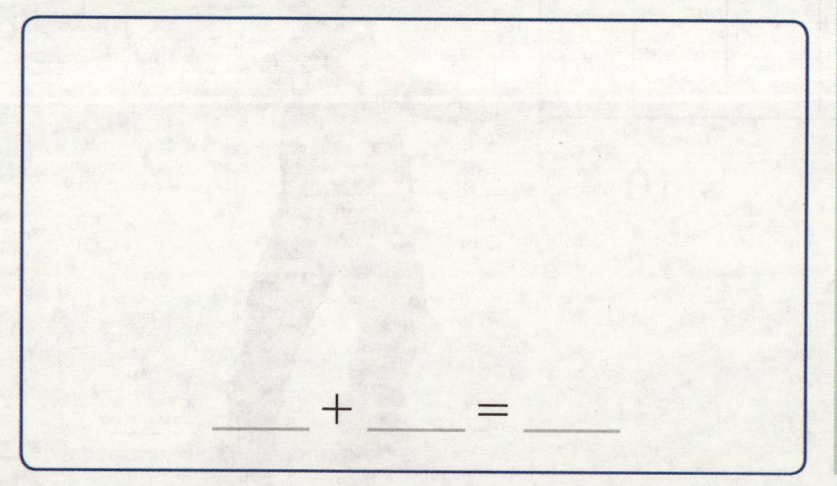

____ + ____ = ____

10. Assessment Todd's team has 5 soccer balls. Todd's coach brings some more. Todd's team now has 10 soccer balls.

Which addition fact shows how many soccer balls Todd's coach brought?

Ⓐ 5 + 5 = 10

Ⓑ 10 + 3 = 13

Ⓒ 7 + 3 = 10

Ⓓ 10 + 7 = 17

Name _____

Homework & Practice 2-4
Facts with 5 on a Ten-Frame

Another Look! You can write an addition fact with 5 using a ten-frame. You can also write an addition fact for 10 using a ten-frame.

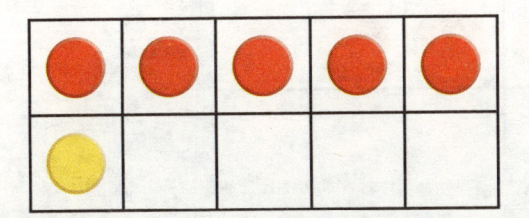

$5 + 1 = 6$

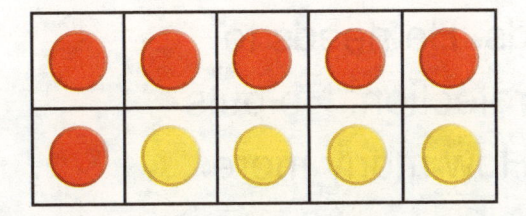

$6 + 4 = \underline{10}$

HOME ACTIVITY Play a game using ten-frames drawn on a sheet of paper. Draw circles on each ten-frame. Then ask your child to write an accompanying equation using 5 or 10 below each ten-frame.

Look at the ten-frames.
Write an addition fact with 5.
Then write an addition fact for 10.

1. 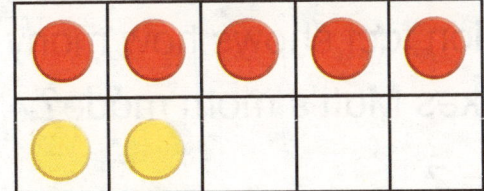 $5 + 2 = \underline{}$

   $\underline{} + \underline{} = 10$

2. 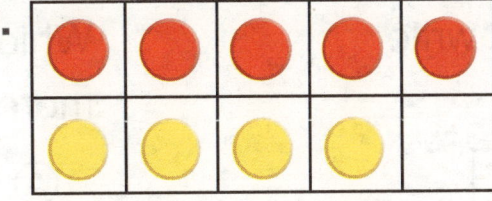 $5 + 4 = \underline{}$

   $\underline{} + \underline{} = 10$

3. 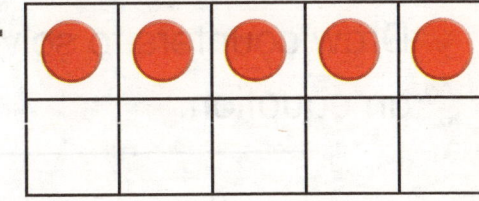 $5 + 0 = \underline{}$

   $\underline{} + \underline{} = 10$

Topic 2 | Lesson 4

Look for Patterns Write an addition fact with 5. Then write an addition fact for 10.

4. 5 + ___ = ___

   6 + ___ = 10

5. 5 + ___ = ___

   9 + ___ = 10

6. 5 + ___ = ___

   8 + ___ = 10

7. **Math and Science** Rich is going rock climbing with his friends. He needs to pack 10 helmets for protection. He puts 4 helmets in the van. How many more helmets does Rich need to pack?

   Draw counters to solve. Then write an equation.

   ___ + ___ = ___   ___ helmets

8. **Higher Order Thinking** A camp has 7 tents in all. First, the campers set up 5 tents. How many more tents did the campers set up?

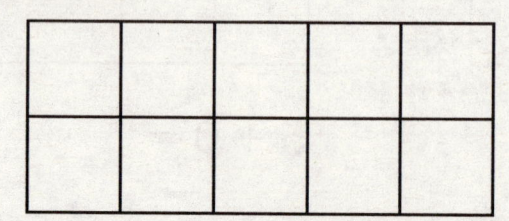

   Draw counters to solve. Then write an equation.

   ___ = ___ + ___   ___ tents

9. **Assessment** Matt's mom makes 10 pancakes in all. First, she makes 6 pancakes. Then she makes some more.

   Which addition fact shows how many more pancakes Matt's mom made?

   Ⓐ 6 + 1 = 7

   Ⓑ 6 + 4 = 10

   Ⓒ 10 + 4 = 14

   Ⓓ 6 + 6 = 12

102 one hundred two

Topic 2 | Lesson 4

Name _____

Solve & Share

Write an addition equation for the green and yellow cubes in each cube tower. How are the addition equations the same? How are they different?

Lesson 2-5
Add in Any Order

I can ...
use the same addends to write two different equations with the same sum.

I can also make math arguments.

___ + ___ = ___   ___ + ___ = ___

4 and 2 is 6.

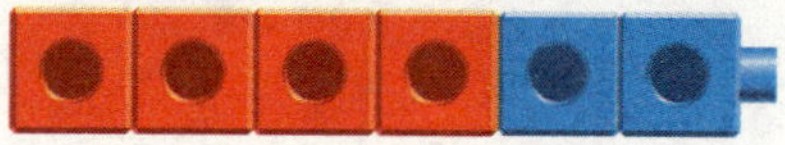

2 and 4 is 6.

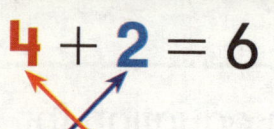

$4 + 2 = 6$

$2 + 4 = 6$

4 plus 2 equals 6.
2 plus 4 equals 6.

$$\begin{array}{r}4\\+2\\\hline 6\end{array} \qquad \begin{array}{r}2\\+4\\\hline 6\end{array}$$

You can change the order of the addends. The sum is the same.

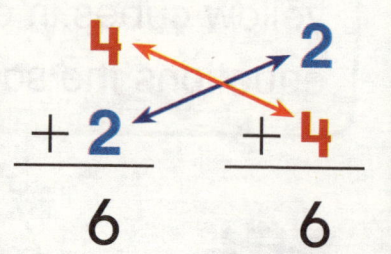

You can write 2 addition equations.

Do You Understand?

Show Me! How can you use cubes to show that $5 + 3$ is the same as $3 + 5$?

Guided Practice

Color to change the order of the addends. Then write the addition equations.

1. $3 + 4 = 7$

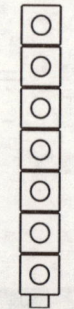

   ___ + ___ = ___

2. ___ + ___ = ___

   ___ + ___ = ___

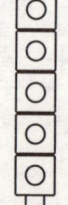

Name _____

Independent Practice Write the sum. Then change the order of the addends. Write the new addition equation.

3. 2 + 3 = ___
   ___ + ___ = ___

4. 1 + 6 = ___
   ___ + ___ = ___

5. ___ = 3 + 6
   ___ = ___ + ___

6. 5 + 2 = ___
   ___ + ___ = ___

7. 4 + 5 = ___
   ___ + ___ = ___

8. 6 + 2 = ___
   ___ + ___ = ___

Number Sense Use the numbers on the cards to write two addition equations.

9. [3] [8] [5]

   ___ + ___ = ___
   ___ + ___ = ___

10. [4] [6] [2]

    ___ = ___ + ___
    ___ = ___ + ___

Topic 2 | Lesson 5

Problem Solving Solve each problem below.

11. **Model** Liza and Anna collect 6 cans on Monday. On Tuesday, they collect 4 cans. How many cans did they collect in all?

Draw a picture. Then write two different addition equations.

___ + ___ = ___

___ + ___ = ___

12. **Higher Order Thinking** Draw a picture of 5 birds. Make some blue. Make the rest red.

Write two addition equations to tell about the picture.

___ + ___ = ___

___ + ___ = ___

13. **Assessment** Look at the two addition equations. Which is the missing addend?

$9 = \underline{?} + 2$

$9 = 2 + \underline{?}$

Ⓐ 6
Ⓑ 7
Ⓒ 8
Ⓓ 9

Both equations have a 2 and a 9.

Name _____

Homework & Practice 2-5
Add in Any Order

Another Look! When you change the order of addends, the sum is the same.

$4 + 2 = 6$

$2 + 4 = 6$

$5 + 2 = 7$

$2 + 5 = 7$

HOME ACTIVITY Write several addition equations for your child. Have him or her change the order of addends and write the new addition equation. Ask, "How are the addition equations the same? How are they different?"

Add. Write addition equations with addends in a different order.

1. ___ + ___ = ___   ___ + ___ = ___

Look for Patterns Write two addition equations for each cube train.

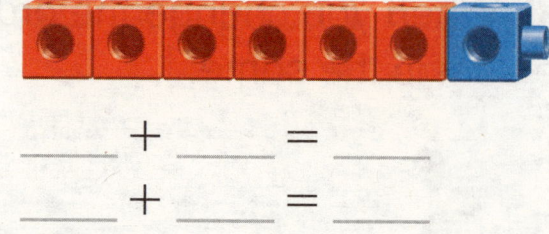

2. ___ + ___ = ___
   ___ + ___ = ___

3. ___ + ___ = ___
   ___ + ___ = ___

4. **Higher Order Thinking** Use the cubes below. Pick two colors of cubes. Write an addition story. Then write two addition equations for your story.

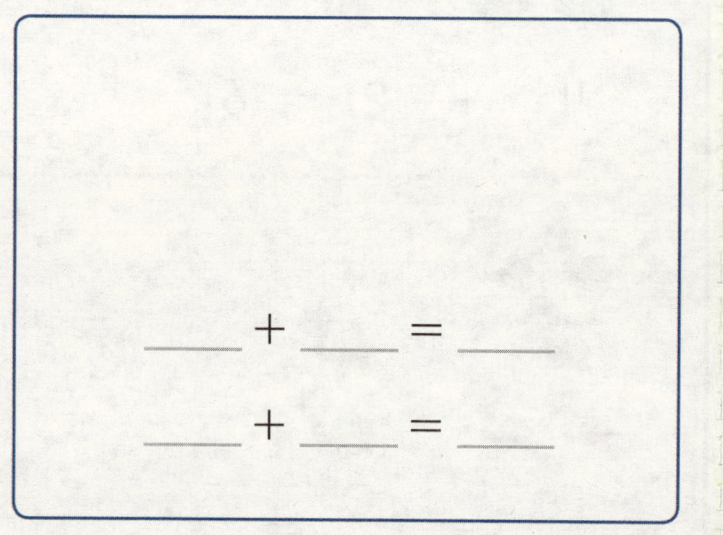

   ___ + ___ = ___
   ___ + ___ = ___

5. **Assessment** Which shows two ways to add the cubes in the cube train?

   Ⓐ 4 + 3, 3 + 4
   Ⓑ 2 + 6, 6 + 2
   Ⓒ 2 + 7, 7 + 2
   Ⓓ 5 + 2, 2 + 5

6. **Assessment** Which has the same value as 5 + 1?

   Ⓐ 1 + 2
   Ⓑ 5 + 3
   Ⓒ 2 + 6
   Ⓓ 1 + 5

108 one hundred eight

Topic 2 | Lesson 5

Name _____

Solve & Share

There are 5 people on a bus. It stops and 2 people get off. Use the number line to show how many people are still on the bus. Write the number.

Lesson 2-6
Count Back to Subtract

I can ...
count back to solve subtraction problems.

I can also model with math.

←—|—|—|—|—|—|—|—|—|—|—→
0 1 2 3 4 5 6 7 8 9 10

_____ people are left on the bus.

Topic 2 | Lesson 6 — one hundred nine — 109

You can use the number line to help you subtract.

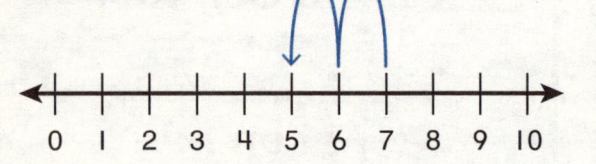

0 1 2 3 4 5 6 7 8 9 10

7, 6, 5   7 − 2 = 5

If I start at 7 and count back 2, I end at 5.

When you subtract 3, you count back 3.

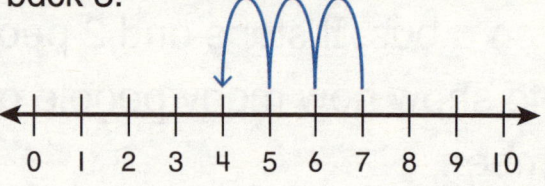

0 1 2 3 4 5 6 7 8 9 10

7, 6, 5, 4

$$\begin{array}{r} 7 \\ -3 \\ \hline 4 \end{array}$$

When you subtract 0, you count back 0.

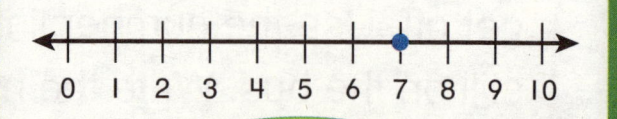

0 1 2 3 4 5 6 7 8 9 10

$$\begin{array}{r} 7 \\ -0 \\ \hline 7 \end{array}$$

If I start at 7 and don't count back any, I stay at 7!

Do You Understand?

Show Me! Write subtraction equations to show counting back by 1, 2, or 3.

Guided Practice
Count back to complete each subtraction fact.

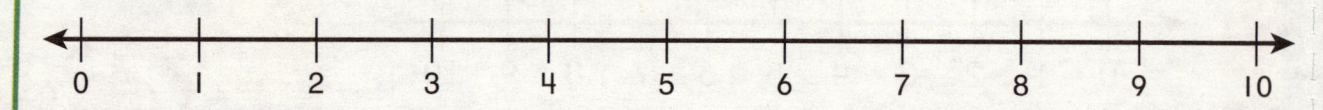

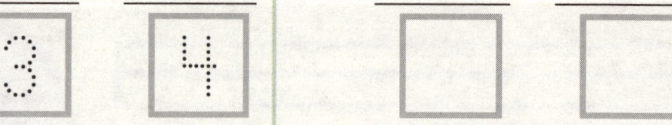

0 1 2 3 4 5 6 7 8 9 10

1. $\begin{array}{r} 4 \\ -1 \\ \hline 3 \end{array}$ $\begin{array}{r} 4 \\ -0 \\ \hline 4 \end{array}$

2. $\begin{array}{r} 6 \\ -0 \\ \hline \end{array}$ $\begin{array}{r} 6 \\ -2 \\ \hline \end{array}$

3. $\begin{array}{r} 9 \\ -5 \\ \hline \end{array}$ $\begin{array}{r} 9 \\ -3 \\ \hline \end{array}$

Name _____

Independent Practice — Complete each subtraction fact. Count back or use the number line to help you.

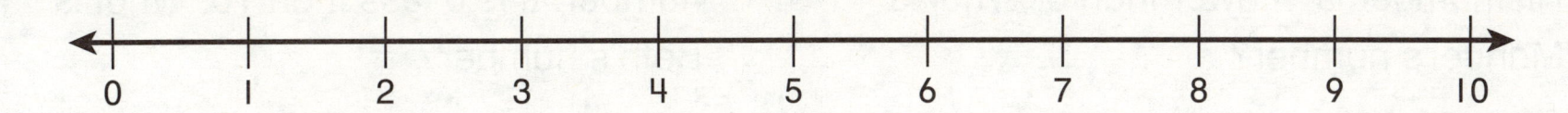

```
←—|—|—|—|—|—|—|—|—|—|—→
  0 1 2 3 4 5 6 7 8 9 10
```

4. 6
   −5
   ☐

5. 8
   −0
   ☐

6. 10
   −8
   ☐

7. 7
   −3
   ☐

8. 9
   −4
   ☐

Draw a picture to solve. Write a subtraction equation.

9. **Higher Order Thinking** Amy and Ryan buy pencils at the store. Amy buys 10 pencils. Ryan buys 8 pencils. How many fewer pencils did Ryan buy?

____ − ____ = ____ fewer pencils

Topic 2 | Lesson 6

Problem Solving Solve each problem below. Write a subtraction equation to match the problem.

10. **Reasoning** Manuel picks a number. His number is 4 fewer than 8. What is Manuel's number?

    ___ − ___ = ___

    Manuel's number is ___.

11. **Reasoning** Beth is thinking of a number. It is 0 less than 10. What is Beth's number?

    ___ − ___ = ___

    Beth's number is ___.

12. **Higher Order Thinking** Complete the subtraction equation. Then write a story to match the equation.

    5 − 1 = ___

    _____
    _____
    _____

13. **✓ Assessment** Jan has 10 tickets. She gives 2 tickets to her friends. How many tickets does Jan have left?

    Ⓐ 8
    Ⓑ 6
    Ⓒ 4
    Ⓓ 2

    You can write an equation to help you solve the problem.

Name _____

Homework & Practice 2-6
Count Back to Subtract

Another Look! You can count back to solve subtraction problems.

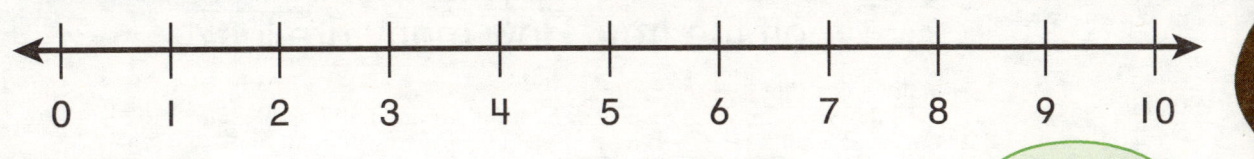

$4 - 2 = ?$
Start at 4.
Count back 2. **4**, 3, 2
Solve the problem.
$4 - 2 = 2$

$6 - 1 = ?$
Start at 6.
Count back 1. **6,** 5
Solve the problem.
$6 - 1 = 5$

Count back to subtract.

HOME ACTIVITY Using a collection of objects such as counters, count out 6. Then have your child tell what 2 less than 6 equals. Ask, "What subtraction equation did you make?" Continue with other subtraction facts, having your child subtract 0, 1, or 2.

Count back or use a number line to help you subtract.

1. (basket with 9)
Count back 1.   Solve the problem.
_____ $9 - 1 =$ _____

2. (purse with 10)
Count back 0.   Solve the problem.
_____ $10 - 0 =$ _____

Topic 2 | Lesson 6   Digital Resources at SavvasRealize.com   one hundred thirteen   **113**

Write a subtraction equation for each story.

3. There are 9 apples in Maya's basket. She eats 1 apple. How many apples are left?

___ − ___ = ___

4. There are 6 cups on a tray. 4 cups fall off the tray. How many are left?

___ − ___ = ___

5. **Higher Order Thinking** Write a subtraction equation. Then write a story to match your equation.

___ = ___ − ___

6. **Assessment** Nicole has 8 pages to read in her book. She reads 3 pages on the bus. Which equation shows how many pages Nicole has left to read?

Ⓐ $10 - 5 = 5$
Ⓑ $10 - 2 = 8$
Ⓒ $8 - 2 = 6$
Ⓓ $8 - 3 = 5$

Name _____

Solve & Share

Jenna has 6 beachballs. 4 of them blow to the other side of the pool. How many does she have left?

How can you use an addition fact to find the answer to 6 − 4 = ____? Use counters to help you solve the problem.

Lesson 2-7
Think Addition to Subtract

I can ...
use addition facts I know to help me solve subtraction problems.

I can also look for patterns.

____ + ____ = ____   So, ____ − ____ = ____.

Topic 2 | Lesson 7 · one hundred fifteen · 115

You can use addition to help you subtract.

$7 - 3 = \boxed{?}$

$3 + \boxed{?} = 7$

"What can I add to 3 to make 7?"

$3 + \boxed{4} = 7$

"The missing part is 4."

Think of the addition fact to solve the subtraction equation.

$7 - 3 = \boxed{4}$

"$3 + 4 = 7$"

Do You Understand?

Show Me! How can an addition fact help you solve $7 - 6$?

Guided Practice

Think addition to help you subtract. Draw the missing part. Then write the numbers.

1.
$5 - 4 = ?$
$4 + \underline{\quad} = 5$
So, $5 - 4 = \underline{\quad}$.

2.
$6 - 5 = ?$
$5 + \underline{\quad} = 6$
So, $6 - 5 = \underline{\quad}$.

Independent Practice

Think addition to help you subtract. Draw the missing part. Then write the numbers.

3. [8]

6 + ___ = 8

So, 8 − 6 = ___.

4. [7]

4 + ___ = 7

So, 7 − 4 = ___.

5. [4]

3 + ___ = 4

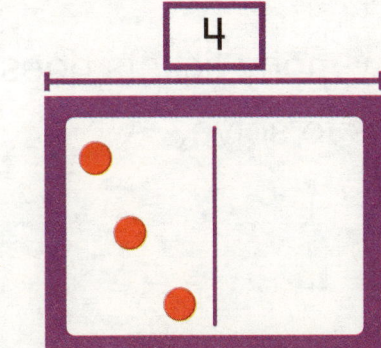

So, 4 − 3 = ___.

6. **Higher Order Thinking** Draw the shape to complete the equation.

If ⬤ + ▲ = ⬛,

then ⬛ − ⬤ = ___.

Problem Solving Write an addition and a subtraction equation to solve.

7. **Use Tools** Pam needs 8 tickets to get on a ride. She has 2 tickets. She needs some more tickets.

   How many tickets does Pam still need? You can use tools to solve.

   ____ + ____ = ____

   ____ − ____ = ____

   ____ tickets

   Which tool could help you solve this problem?

8. **Higher Order Thinking** Kathy has a box that holds 6 crayons. 4 crayons are inside the box. She uses addition to find how many are missing. Is Kathy correct? Explain.

   $6 + 4 = 10$
   10 crayons are missing.

9. **Assessment** Which addition facts can help you solve the problem? Choose all that apply.

   $9 - 2 = ?$

   ☐ $7 + 2 = 9$

   ☐ $5 + 4 = 9$

   ☐ $2 + 7 = 9$

   ☐ $8 + 1 = 9$

Name _____

Homework & Practice 2-7
Think Addition to Subtract

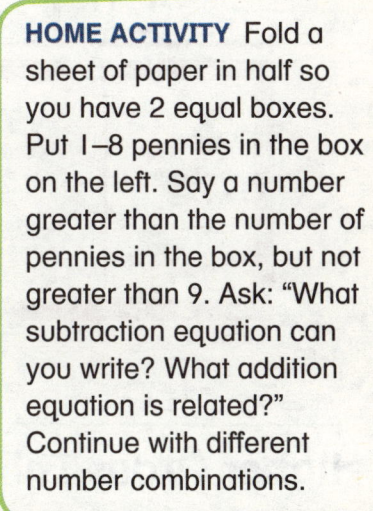

Another Look! Use addition to help you subtract.

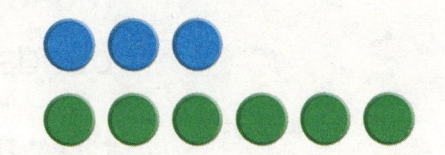

I know that
2 + 6 = 8.
So, 8 − 6 = 2.

3 + 6 = 9

So, 9 − 6 = 3.

HOME ACTIVITY Fold a sheet of paper in half so you have 2 equal boxes. Put 1–8 pennies in the box on the left. Say a number greater than the number of pennies in the box, but not greater than 9. Ask: "What subtraction equation can you write? What addition equation is related?" Continue with different number combinations.

Write an addition fact that will help you write and solve the subtraction fact.

1. ___ + ___ = ___

___ − ___ = ___

2. ___ + ___ = ___

___ − ___ = ___

3. ___ + ___ = ___

___ − ___ = ___

Write a subtraction and an addition equation to solve.

4. **Look for Patterns** Draw counters.

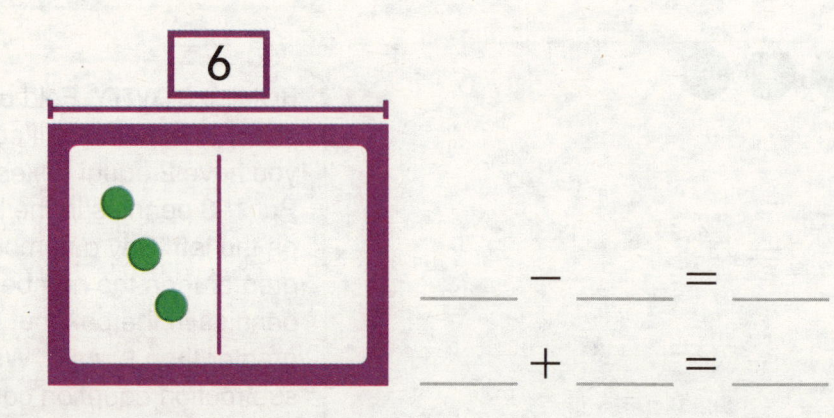

   [6]

   ___ − ___ = ___

   ___ + ___ = ___

5. **Reasoning** Rosi buys 10 beads to make a bracelet. She buys 3 blue beads and some white beads.

   How many white beads does Rosi buy?

   ___ white beads

   ___ + ___ = ___

   ___ − ___ = ___

Higher Order Thinking Draw the shapes to complete each equation.

6. If △ + ○ = □,

   then ___ − ___ = ___.

7. If ▭ = ▭ + ▭,

   then ___ = ___ − ___.

8. **Assessment** Tia and Sue make 8 baskets. If Sue makes 2 baskets, how many baskets does Tia make?

   Which addition facts can help you subtract? Choose all that apply.

   ☐ 8 + 6 = 14
   ☐ 2 + 8 = 10
   ☐ 6 + 2 = 8
   ☐ 2 + 6 = 8

Name _____

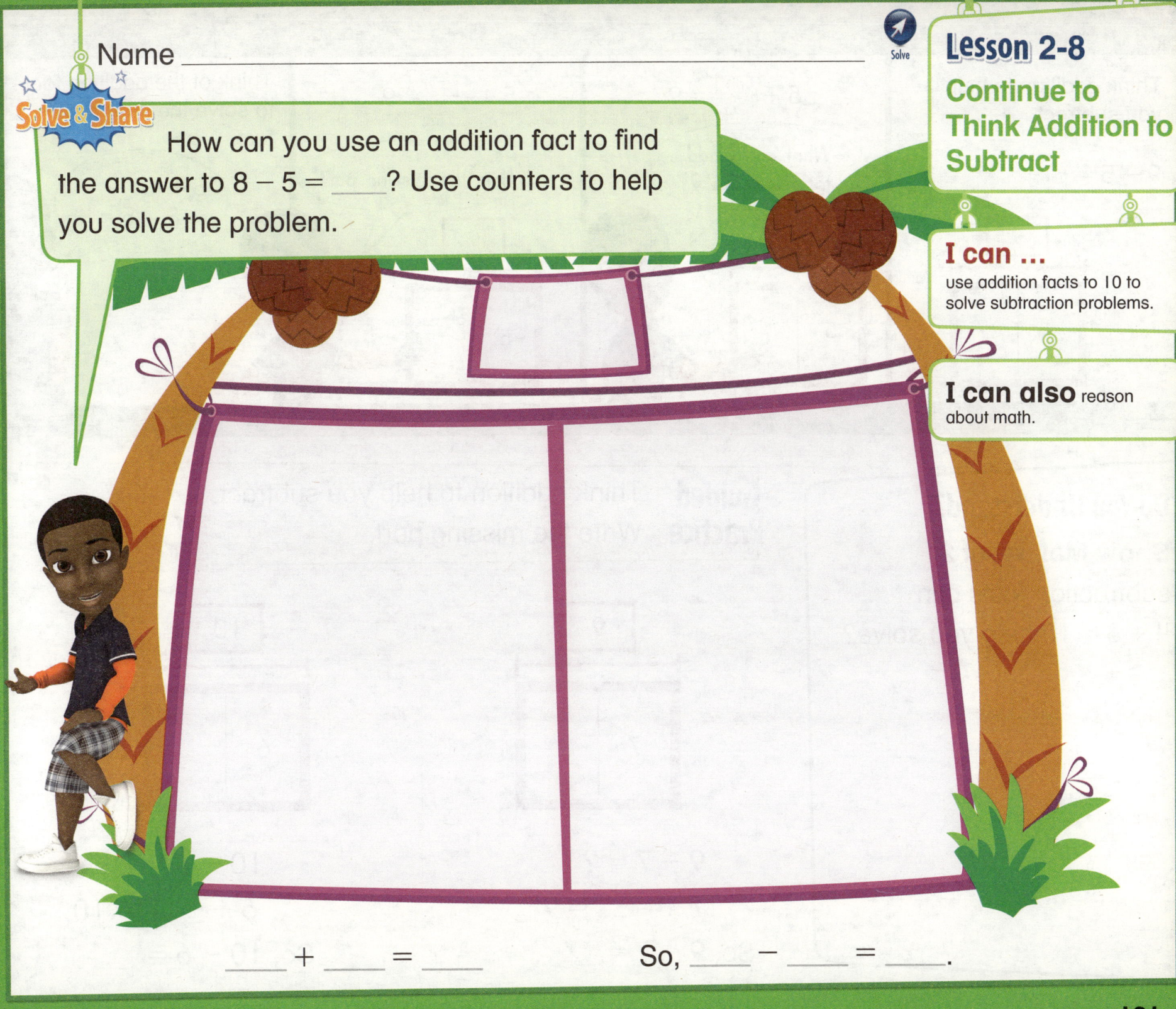

Lesson 2-8

Continue to Think Addition to Subtract

Solve & Share

How can you use an addition fact to find the answer to 8 − 5 = ___? Use counters to help you solve the problem.

I can ...
use addition facts to 10 to solve subtraction problems.

I can also reason about math.

___ + ___ = ___   So, ___ − ___ = ___.

Topic 2 | Lesson 8   one hundred twenty-one   **121**

Think addition to help you subtract.

$9 - 5 = \boxed{?}$

9	
5	?

$5 + \boxed{?} = 9$

"What can I add to 5 to make 9?"

9	
5	?

$5 + \boxed{4} = 9$

"4 is the missing part."

9	
5	4

Think of the addition fact to solve the subtraction fact.

"$5 + 4 = 9$, so $9 - 5 = 4$."

Do You Understand?

Show Me! What 2 subtraction facts can $4 + 6 = 10$ help you solve?

Guided Practice

Think addition to help you subtract. Write the missing part.

1.
9	
7	2

$9 - 7 = ?$
$7 + \underline{2} = 9$
So, $9 - 7 = \underline{2}$.

2.
10	
6	

$10 - 6 = ?$
$6 + \underline{} = 10$
So, $10 - 6 = \underline{}$.

Name _____

Independent Practice
Think addition to help you subtract. Write the missing part.

3. [8]
    | 2 | |

    $2 + \underline{\quad} = 8$

    So, $8 - 2 = \underline{\quad}$.

4. [6]
    | 3 | |

    $3 + \underline{\quad} = 6$

    So, $6 - 3 = \underline{\quad}$.

5. [9]
    | 2 | |

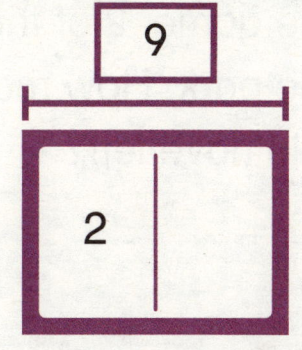

    $2 + \underline{\quad} = 9$

    So, $9 - 2 = \underline{\quad}$.

6. **Math and Science** Turtles have shells to protect them from dangers in the ocean. 10 turtles are on the beach. Then some turtles swim away. Now there are 7 turtles on the beach. How many turtles swam away?

Write an addition and a subtraction equation to match the story.

$\underline{\quad} + \underline{\quad} = \underline{\quad}$

$\underline{\quad} - \underline{\quad} = \underline{\quad}$ $\underline{\quad}$ turtles

You can think addition to help you subtract!

Topic 2 | Lesson 8

Problem Solving Solve each subtraction story. Write a related addition fact to help you subtract.

7. **Generalize** Jamie brings 7 baseballs to the game. 2 of the balls are hit out of the park. How many baseballs does Jamie have left?

___ + ___ = ___

___ − ___ = ___

___ baseballs

8. **Generalize** The Purple team scores 5 points. The Green team scores 9 points. How many more points does the Green team score than the Purple team?

___ + ___ = ___

___ − ___ = ___

___ points

9. **Higher Order Thinking** Write a subtraction story about the fish.

_____

_____

___ ◯ ___ = ___

___ ◯ ___ = ___

10. **Assessment** Mrs. Kane has 9 students. Some are drawing pictures. 6 are reading books. How many students are drawing pictures?

Which addition facts can you use to find the answer? Choose all that apply.

☐ 3 + 5 = 8
☐ 3 + 6 = 9
☐ 6 + 3 = 9
☐ 4 + 6 = 10

124 one hundred twenty-four

Topic 2 | Lesson 8

Homework & Practice 2-8
Continue to Think Addition to Subtract

Another Look! You can use addition facts to help you subtract. Look at the subtraction fact. Then look at the addition fact that can help.

9 − 1 = 8

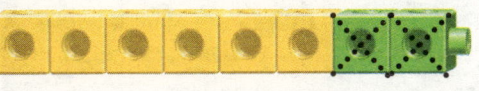

8 + 1 = 9

8 − 2 = 6

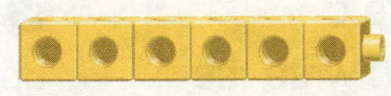

6 + 2 = 8

HOME ACTIVITY Give your child a subtraction fact to solve. Have him or her use pennies or other objects, such as counters, to solve the problem. Then have your child tell you the addition problem that is related. Continue with several subtraction facts.

Subtract. Then write the addition fact that helped you subtract.

1.  10 − ___ = 8
   8 + ___ = 10

2.  9 − ___ = 5
   5 + ___ = 9

3.  8 − ___ = 1
   1 + ___ = 8

Think addition to help you subtract. Write the missing part.

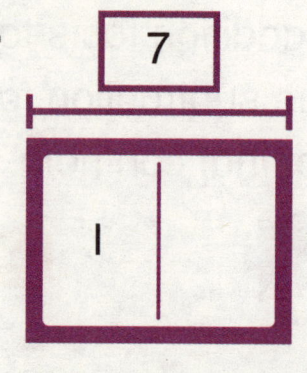

4.

6

4

$4 + \underline{} = 6$

So, $6 - 4 = \underline{}$.

5.

7

1

$1 + \underline{} = 7$

So, $7 - 1 = \underline{}$.

6. Higher Order Thinking Write a number story for $10 - 3$. Then write the addition fact that helped you subtract.

7. Assessment Miguel and Andy pick apples. Miguel picks 9 apples. Andy picks 4 apples. How many fewer apples did Andy pick than Miguel?

Which addition facts can help you solve this number story? Choose all that apply.

☐ $5 + 4 = 9$
☐ $4 + 4 = 8$
☐ $6 + 3 = 9$
☐ $4 + 5 = 9$

Topic 2 | Lesson 8

Name _____

Lesson 2-9

Solve Word Problems with Facts to 10

6 fish swim by. Some more fish join them. Now there are 10 fish. How many fish joined the fish swimming by?

Draw a picture to solve the problem. Then write an equation.

I can ...
draw pictures and write equations to help solve word problems.

I can also make sense of problems.

___ + ___ = ___

Topic 2 | Lesson 9 — one hundred twenty-seven — 127

Slater has 7 books. He gives some books to Anna. Now Slater has 2 books. How many books did he give Anna?

You can write an equation to model the problem.

7 − ___?___ = 2

Slater's books minus the books he gives Anna equals 2. So, Slater gives Anna 5 books.

You can also count back from 7 to 2 to solve.

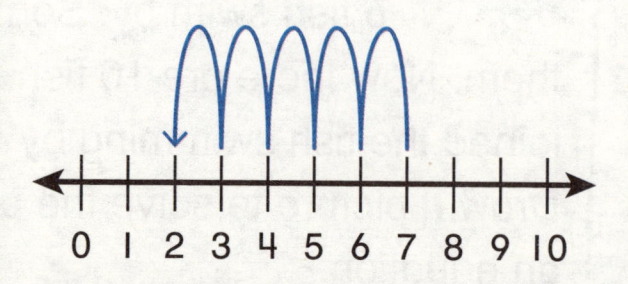

0 1 2 3 4 5 6 7 8 9 10

Count each jump from 7 when you count back. There are 5 jumps.

Do You Understand?

Show Me! 7 cubes are on a table. Some cubes fall on the floor. Now there are 3 cubes on the table. How many fell on the floor?

Guided Practice

Draw a picture. Then write an addition or a subtraction equation.

1. Maria sees 3 blue birds. Then she sees some red birds. Maria sees 9 birds in all. How many red birds did Maria see?

___ ◯ ___ = ___

128 one hundred twenty-eight

Topic 2 | Lesson 9

Name _____

Independent Practice
Draw a picture. Then write an addition or a subtraction equation.

2. Jamal picks 9 berries. Then Ed picks more berries. Jamal and Ed pick 12 berries in all. How many berries did Ed pick?

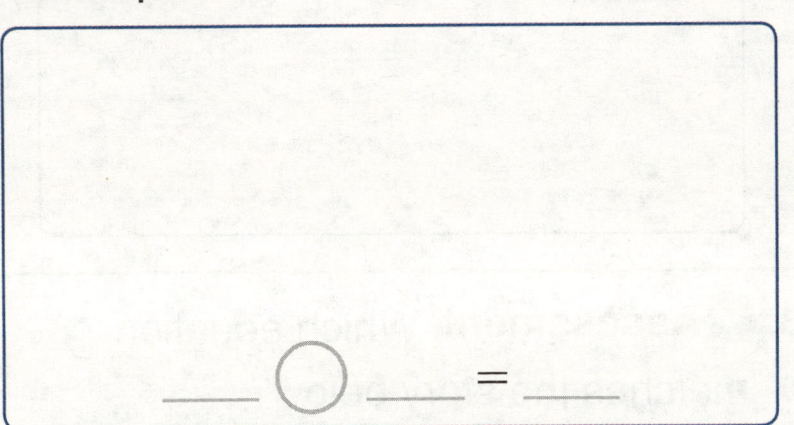

___ ◯ ___ = ___

3. There are 8 flowers in Vicky's garden. She picks some flowers. Now there are 4 flowers in Vicky's garden. How many flowers did Vicky pick?

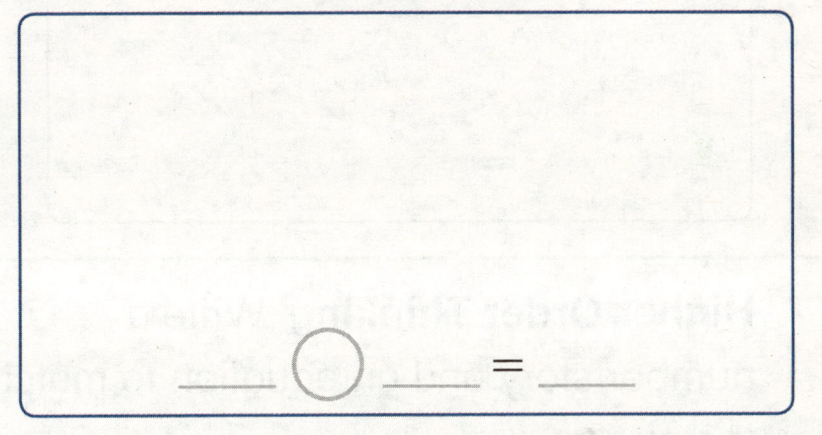

___ ◯ ___ = ___

4. **Higher Order Thinking** Write a number story to match the picture. Then write an equation.

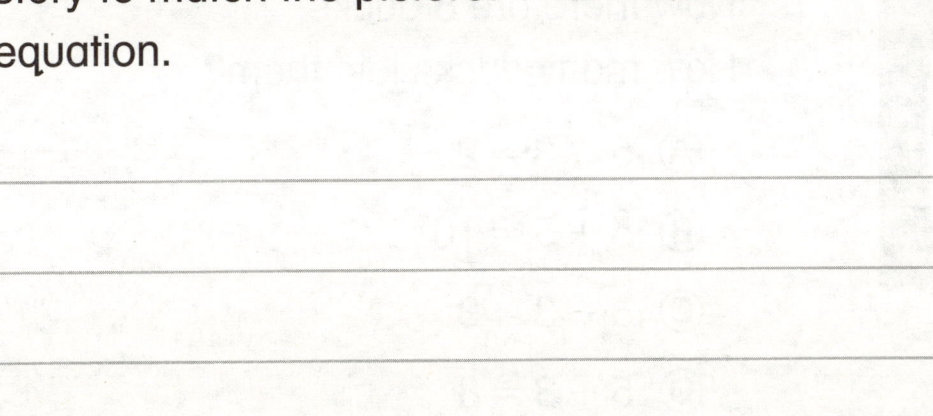

_____
_____
_____

___ = ___ ◯ ___

Topic 2 | Lesson 9

one hundred twenty-nine 129

Problem Solving Draw a picture to help make sense of the problem. Then write an addition or a subtraction equation.

5. **Make Sense** Charlie draws 7 stars. Joey draws 4 stars. How many fewer stars did Joey draw than Charlie?

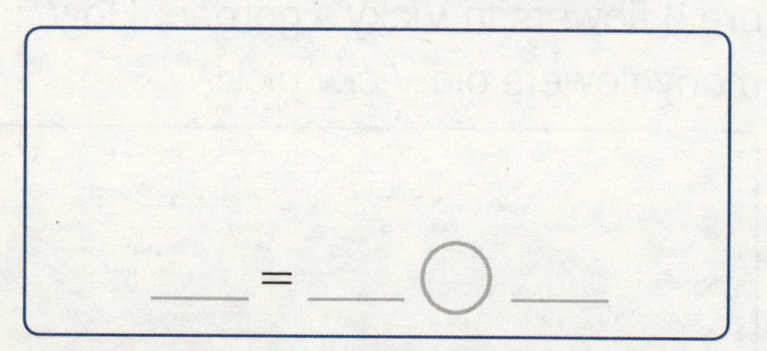

___ = ___ ◯ ___

6. **Make Sense** Brian finds 3 rocks on Monday. He finds 7 rocks on Friday. How many more rocks did Brian find on Friday than on Monday?

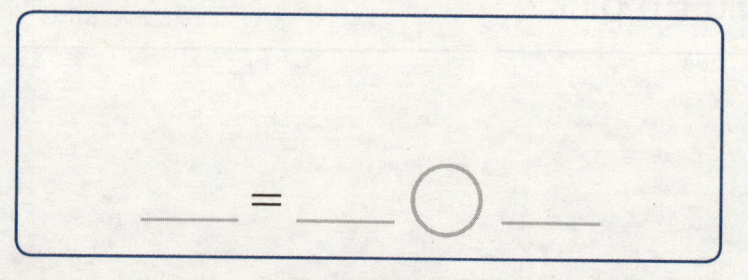

___ = ___ ◯ ___

7. **Higher Order Thinking** Write a number story and an equation to match the picture.

_____
_____
_____
_____

8. **Assessment** Which equation matches the story below?

5 ducks are in a row.
More ducks join them.
Now there are 8 ducks.
How many ducks join them?

Ⓐ $5 - 3 = 2$
Ⓑ $5 + 5 = 10$
Ⓒ $6 - 3 = 3$
Ⓓ $5 + 3 = 8$

Name _____

Homework & Practice 2-9
Solve Word Problems with Facts to 10

Another Look! You can use pictures to solve a number story.

Linda has 4 buttons.
She buys some more.
Now Linda has 7 buttons.

How many buttons did Linda buy?

$4 + 3 = 7$

$\underline{3}$ buttons

HOME ACTIVITY Tell your child a story that involves adding or subtracting. Say, "Draw a picture and write an equation for this story." Check to make sure the drawing and the equation match the story. Repeat with 1 or 2 different stories.

Draw a picture to solve. Then write an equation to match.

1. Abby has 6 apples. Judy has 9 apples.

   How many more apples does Judy have?

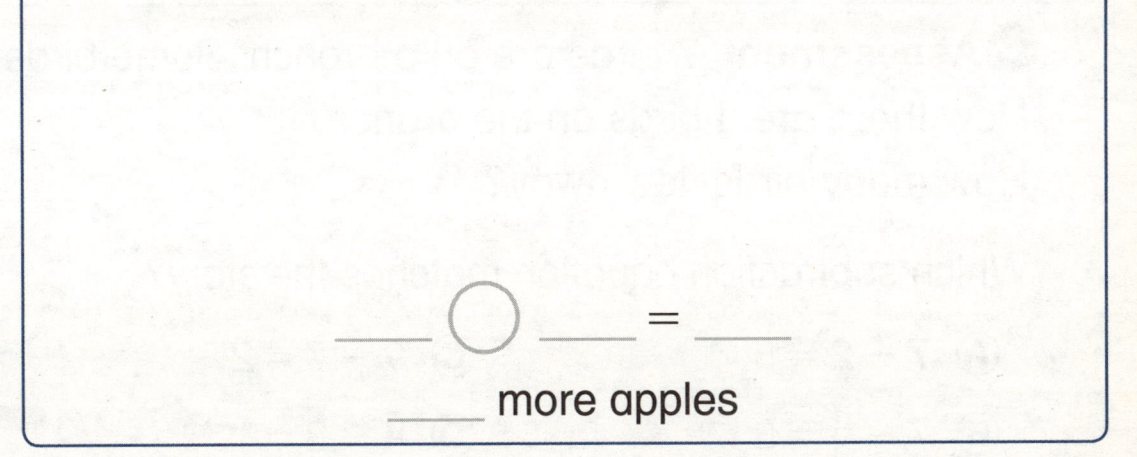

   ___ ○ ___ = ___

   ___ more apples

Topic 2 | Lesson 9   one hundred thirty-one   **131**

Write an equation to solve each problem below.

2. Tim has 9 pears.
   3 pears are yellow.
   The rest are green.
   How many pears are green?

   ___ ◯ ___ = ___

3. Ian has 5 red balloons.
   Max has 6 blue balloons.
   How many balloons do the
   boys have in all?

   ___ ◯ ___ = ___

4. **Higher Order Thinking** Use the chart. Write a number story. Then write an addition or a subtraction equation to match your story.

Fruit	How Many?
Blueberries	4
Raspberries	6

___ ◯ ___ = ___

5. **Assessment** 7 birds are on a branch. Some birds fly away.
   Now there are 4 birds on the branch.
   How many birds flew away?

   Which subtraction equation matches the story?

   Ⓐ $7 - 2 = 5$ Ⓒ $9 - 7 = 2$

   Ⓑ $7 - 4 = 3$ Ⓓ $4 - 3 = 1$

Name _____

Solve & Share

Use counters and the part-part-whole mat to show different ways to make 10. Write the different ways in the table.

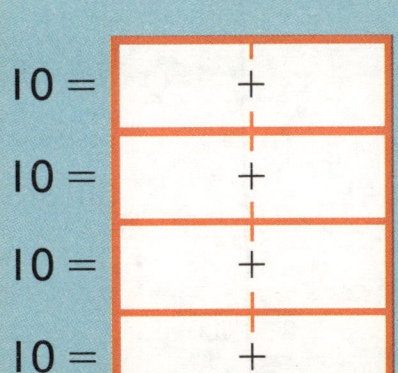

10

Problem Solving

Lesson 2-10
Look For and Use Structure

I can ...
look for patterns and use structure to solve problems.

I can also make 10 in different ways.

10 = ___ + ___
10 = ___ + ___
10 = ___ + ___
10 = ___ + ___

Thinking Habits
Is there a pattern?
How can I describe the pattern?

Topic 2 | Lesson 10 | one hundred thirty-three **133**

The bears and lions want to cross the sea. Only 10 animals can fit on the boat. Show all the ways they can go on the boat.

How can I use structure to help me solve this problem?

Bears	Lions
0	10
1	9

I can look for patterns to help me find how many bears and how many lions.

There is a pattern in the table. The parts in each row add up to 10. As the number of bears increases, the number of lions decreases.

Bears	Lions
0	10
1	9
2	8
3	7
4	6
5	5
6	4
7	3
8	2
9	1
10	0

The table shows all the ways the bears and lions can go on the boat.

Do You Understand?

Show Me! What is a pattern in the table that shows how many bears and how many lions there are?

☆ Guided Practice ☆

Use a pattern to help you solve the problem.

1. Patty has 4 dog stickers and 4 cat stickers. She wants to put 6 stickers on a page of her book.

   Use structure to show 3 different ways Patty can put stickers on the page.

4	2

134 one hundred thirty-four

Topic 2 | Lesson 10

Name _____

Independent Practice

Use a pattern to help you solve each problem.

2. Max has 5 markers. He can put the markers in his desk or in his bag.

Complete the table to show all the ways Max can put the markers away.

Desk	Bag
0	___
___	4
2	3
3	___
___	1
___	___

3. Mrs. Davis fills a box with prizes. She has 7 balls and 7 balloons. She wants to put 10 prizes in the box.

Complete the table to show all the ways Mrs. Davis can fill the box.

7	3
6	4
5	___
4	___
___	___

Use a pattern to help you solve the problem.

4. **Higher Order Thinking** Julie is planting 10 flowers. She can plant them by a tree or in a box. Use structure to help you find 3 different ways Julie can plant the flowers.

___ by a tree and ___ in a box

___ by a tree and ___ in a box

___ by a tree and ___ in a box

Topic 2 | Lesson 10

one hundred thirty-five **135**

Problem Solving

✓ Performance Assessment

Pieces of Fruit

Ed eats 7 pieces of fruit. He can eat strawberries or grapes. Fill in a table to show how many different ways Ed can pick which fruit to eat.

Student A and Student B solved the number story. Each student's table is shown at the right.

5. **Model** Fill in the missing numbers in each table. Use cubes to help you.

Student A	
🍓	🍇
0	
1	
2	
3	
4	
5	
6	
7	

Student B	
🍓	🍇
	6
	1
	4
	3
	2
	5
	0
	7

6. **Look for Patterns** Describe a pattern used in each table.

_____

_____

_____

Name _____

Homework & Practice 2-10
Look For and Use Structure

Another Look! Karen has 5 purple marbles and 4 yellow marbles. She can only fit 5 marbles in her pocket. What are the different ways she can put purple and yellow marbles in her pocket? Use a pattern to help you solve the problem. Then complete the table to show all the ways Karen can put the marbles in her pocket.

The sum of the numbers in each row is __5__.

🟣 Purple	🟡 Yellow
5	0
4	1
3	2
2	3
1	4

HOME ACTIVITY Collect 5 each of two small objects, such as buttons and paperclips. Put 5 buttons in a row. Ask your child, "How many buttons? How many paperclips?" Then replace 1 button with a paperclip and ask the questions again. Continue replacing buttons with paperclips one at a time, asking the questions after each turn. Then ask, "What is the total each time?"

Use structure to find patterns to help you solve the problems below.

1. Tom has 5 toy cars. He can put them away in his toy box or on a shelf. Complete the table to show all the ways Tom can put away his toy cars.

Box	Shelf
5	___
___	1
___	___
2	___
___	4
___	___

2. Kathy has 5 tulips and 5 roses. She wants to plant 5 flowers in her garden. Complete the table to show all the ways Kathy can plant the flowers in her garden.

🌷 Tulips	🌹 Roses
0	___
___	___
___	3
3	___
___	1
5	___

Topic 2 | Lesson 10

Performance Assessment

Making a Fruit Bowl

Bill has 5 apples and 5 bananas. He can only put 5 pieces of fruit in a bowl. How can Bill make a table to show the different ways he can put fruit in the bowl?

🍎	🍌
0	
1	
2	
3	
4	
5	

3. **Generalize** What will be the same in each row of the table?

_____

_____

4. **Reasoning** Will the number of bananas get smaller or larger as you move down the table? How do you know?

_____

_____

5. **Look for Patterns** Write the missing numbers in the table. How do you know your answers are correct?

_____

_____

_____

_____

138 one hundred thirty-eight

Name _____

TOPIC 2 Fluency Practice Activity

Find a Match

Find a partner. Point to a clue. Read the clue.

Look below the clues to find a match. Write the clue letter in the box next to the match.

Find a match for every clue.

I can ...
add and subtract within 10.

Clues

A $3 + 1$

B $8 + 2$

C $4 + 3$

D $2 + 3$

E $1 + 2$

F $5 - 3$

G $9 - 1$

H $5 + 4$

☐ $3 + 2$ ☐ $2 + 8$ ☐ $2 + 1$ ☐ $4 + 5$

☐ $3 + 4$ ☐ $4 - 2$ ☐ $1 + 3$ ☐ $8 - 0$

Answers for *Find a Match* on next page.

Topic 2 | Fluency Practice Activity

TOPIC 2 Vocabulary Review

Word List
- doubles fact
- fewer
- more
- near doubles fact
- number line

Understand Vocabulary

1. Circle the addition equation that is shown on the number line.

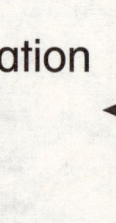

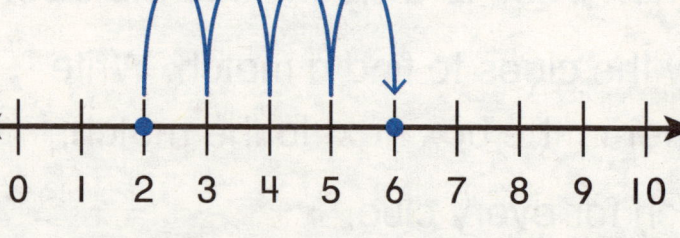

    $1 + 1 = 2$ $2 + 1 = 3$ $2 + 4 = 6$ $3 + 3 = 6$

2. Cross out the parts that do **NOT** show doubles facts.

    $3 + 7$

    $2 + 2$

    $1 + 2$

3. Circle the near doubles facts.

    $4 + 5$

    $2 + 7$

    $3 + 6$

4. Circle the word that completes the sentence. Sam has 6 pens and Bev has 4 pens. Bev has 2 _____ pens than Sam.

    more   red   fewer

Use Vocabulary in Writing

5. Write and solve a story problem. Use at least one term from the Word List.

Answers for Find a Match *on page 139*

C	F	G
D	E	H

Name _____

Set A

Reteaching

There are 8 peppers in the pot. You can add 1 more by counting 1 more.

1 more than 8 is 9.

8 + 1 = 9

Add 1, 2, or 0 to find the sum. Write the addition fact.

1. ___ + ___ = ___

2. ___ + ___ = ___

Set B

You can use doubles facts to add.

2 + 2 = 4

3 + 3 = 6

Both addends are the same. They are doubles.

Write an addition equation for each doubles fact.

3. ___ + ___ = ___

4. How many coins are there in all?

___ + ___ = ___

Topic 2 | Reteaching

Set C

You can use doubles facts to add near doubles.

$2 + 2$

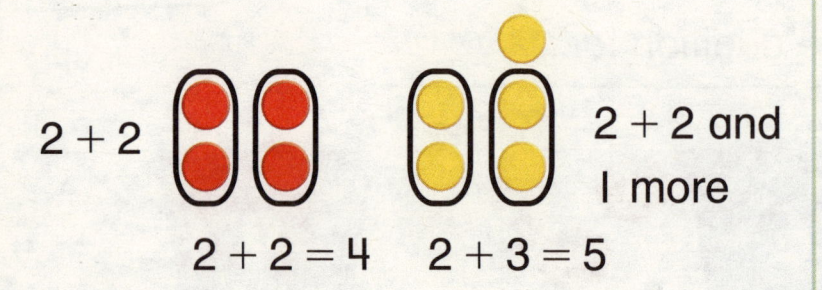

$2 + 2 = 4$

$2 + 2$ and 1 more

$2 + 3 = 5$

Find each sum.

5. 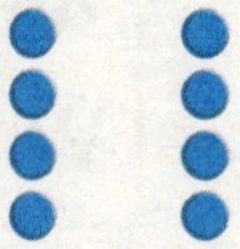 ___ + ___ = ___

___ + ___ = ___

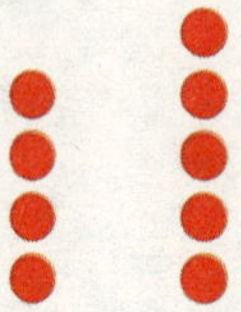

Set D

You can use a ten-frame to learn facts with 5.

Look at the addition equation. Draw counters in the frame.

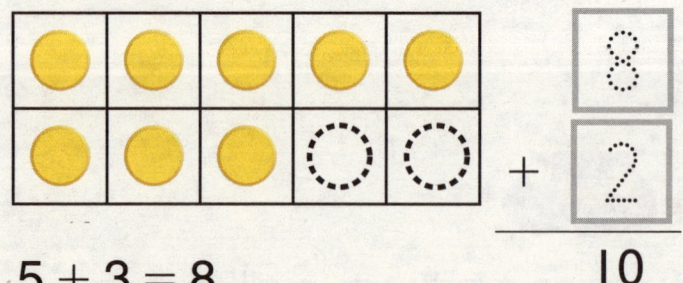

$5 + 3 = 8$

$$\begin{array}{r} 8 \\ + \ 2 \\ \hline 10 \end{array}$$

Draw counters and complete the addition problems.

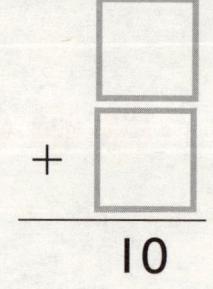

6. 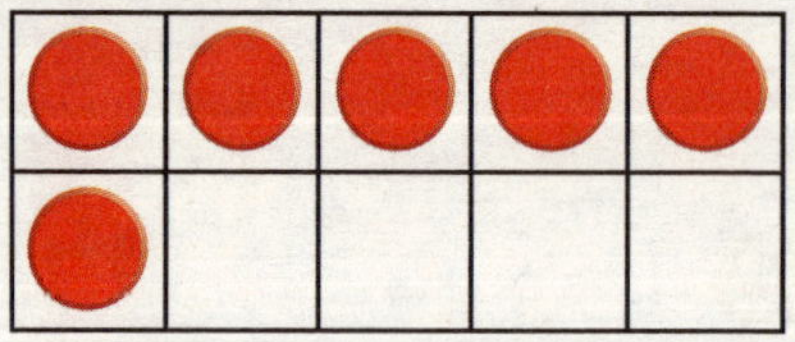 $5 + 1 = $ ___

$$\begin{array}{r} \square \\ + \ \square \\ \hline 10 \end{array}$$

Name _____

Set E

Find the sum.

2 + 5 = 7̲
    sum

You can change the order of the addends.

Write the new addition equation.

5̲ + 2̲ = 7̲
         sum

The sum is the same.

Write the sum. Then change the order of the addends and write a new addition equation.

7. 1 + 4 = ___

___ + ___ = ___

8. 6 + 3 = ___

___ + ___ = ___

When you change the order of the addends, the sum is the same.

Set F

You can subtract by counting back.

2 less than 9 is 7̲.

Write the subtraction fact.

```
  9
- 2
---
  7
```

Count back to find the difference. Write the subtraction fact.

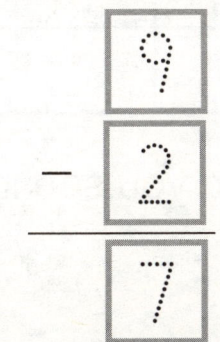

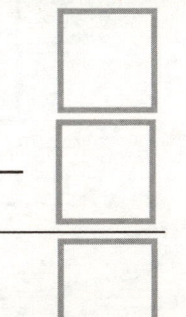

9.
```
  ☐
- ☐
---
  ☐
```
1 less than 4 is ___.

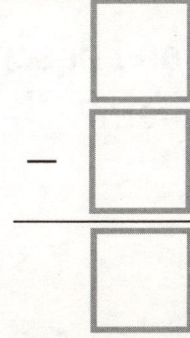

10.
```
  ☐
- ☐
---
  ☐
```
0 less than 6 is ___.

Topic 2 | Reteaching

Set G

You can think addition to help you subtract.

| Think addition to help you subtract. |

8

The missing part is 3.

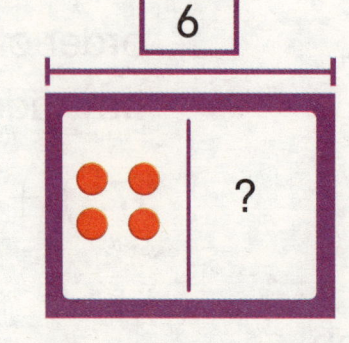

$5 + \underline{3} = 8$

So, $8 - 5 = \underline{3}$.

11. 6

$4 + \underline{} = 6$

So, $6 - 4 = \underline{}$.

12. 7

$6 + \underline{} = 7$

So, $7 - 6 = \underline{}$.

Set H

Thinking Habits

Look For and Use Structure

Is there a pattern?

How can I describe the pattern?

Dani's family can foster 3 animals. She made a list of the number of cats and dogs they can foster.

13. Complete the table below.

Dogs	0	1	2	3
Cats				

14. Describe a pattern you see in the table.

144 one hundred forty-four

Name _____

TOPIC 2 Assessment

1. Molly has 5 toy cars. She got 2 more as a gift. How many toy cars does Molly have now?

    Ⓐ 5
    Ⓑ 6
    Ⓒ 7
    Ⓓ 8

2. Brad has 5 books. His mother gives him 4 more. How many books does Brad have in all?

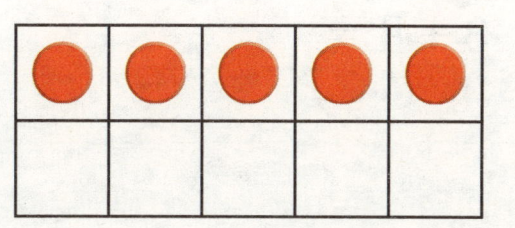

    Ⓐ 1
    Ⓑ 4
    Ⓒ 5
    Ⓓ 9

3. Sammy earns 4 stars in gym class. He earns 3 stars in music class. How many stars did Sammy earn in all? How can you count on to find the answer?

    _____ stars

4. Count back to find the difference. Show your work.

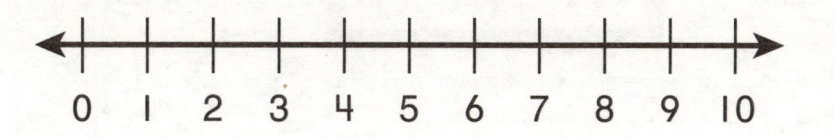

    $8 - 2 = $ _____

Topic 2 | Assessment

one hundred forty-five 145

5. Write the doubles fact that will help you find 3 + 4. Find the missing number.

___ + ___ = ___

3 + 4 = ___

6. Yuri is thinking of a number. His number is 0 less than 9. Use the subtraction equation to find his number.

9 − 0 = ___

7. Find the missing part.

1 + ___ = 6

6 − 1 = ___

8. Which addition equation matches the picture? Choose all that apply.

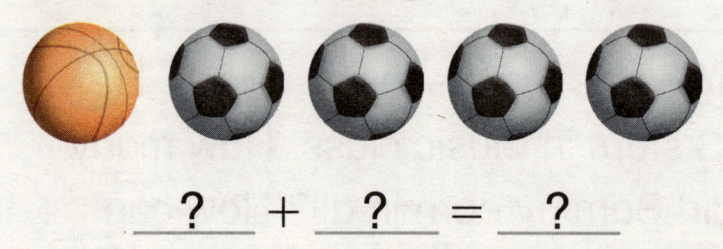

___?___ + ___?___ = ___?___

☐ 1 + 4 = 5

☐ 2 + 2 = 4

☐ 3 + 1 = 4

☐ 4 + 1 = 5

Name _____

9. Which addition equations help you solve $9 - 3$? Choose all that apply.

☐ $6 + 3 = 9$

☐ $9 + 3 = 12$

☐ $3 + 6 = 9$

☐ $9 + 1 = 10$

10. Find $5 + 4$. Use the number line to count on.

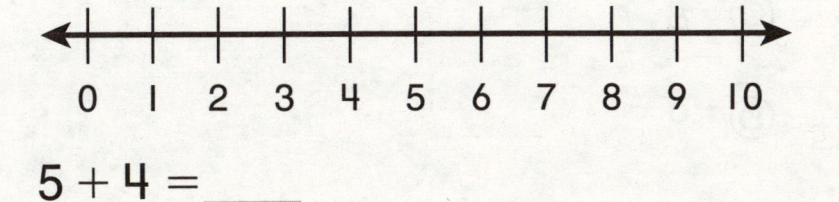

$5 + 4 = $ ___

11. Paul has 5 grapes. His friend gives him 3 more. How many grapes does Paul have in all?

Ⓐ 8

Ⓑ 9

Ⓒ 10

Ⓓ 11

12. 3 frogs sit on a rock. 3 more join them. How many frogs in all? Draw a picture and write an equation.

___ ◯ ___ = ___

___ frogs

13. Add the doubles.
    Find the missing number.

    $4 + 4 =$ ___?___

    Ⓐ 6

    Ⓑ 7

    Ⓒ 8

    Ⓓ 9

14. Erin is thinking of a number. Her number is 5 less than 10. What doubles fact could Erin use to solve the problem?

    $10 - 5 =$ ___?___

    ___ + ___ = ___

15. Think addition to help you subtract. Find the missing part. Write the numbers.

    | 11 |
    | 4 | ? |

    $4 +$ ___ $= 11$

    $11 - 4 =$ ___

16. Tina wants to buy 6 beads. She can buy red or blue beads. Show the different ways she can buy beads. Write the numbers in the table.

Red	___	___	2	3	___	5	___
Blue	6	5	___	___	___	___	0

Name _____

Favorite Fruits

The first-grade students at Park School took a survey of their favorite fruits. They made this chart.

Our Favorite Fruits	
Fruit	Number of Votes
Apple	5
Orange	4
Banana	6
Strawberry	2
Blueberry	3
Cherry	3
Peach	4
Grape	1

TOPIC 2 — Performance Assessment

1. How many fewer students voted for **Strawberry** than **Apple**? Draw a picture and write an equation to solve.

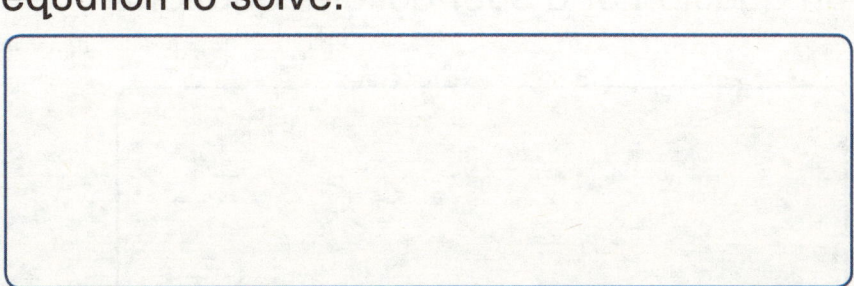

2. Laura says that she can use near doubles to find the total number of votes for **Banana** and **Strawberry**. Do you agree?

   Circle **Yes** or **No**.

   Show your work to explain.

3. 2 girls voted for **Orange**. Some boys voted for **Orange**.
   How many boys voted for **Orange**?

   Draw a picture to solve. Then write an addition or a subtraction equation.

   Write how many boys voted for **Orange**.

   _____

4. Fewer girls voted for **Banana** than boys. Complete the chart. Show the different ways boys and girls could have voted.

Girls	Boys

5. Gina says that **Blueberry** and **Orange** have the same total number of votes as **Cherry** and **Peach**. Is she correct? Explain how you know.

TOPIC 3
Addition Facts to 20: Use Strategies

Essential Question: What strategies can you use for adding to 20?

Some animals have special teeth to eat plants.

Some animals have special teeth to eat meat.

Wow! Let's do this project and learn more.

Math and Science Project: What Do They Eat?

Find Out Talk to friends and relatives about the things different animals eat. Ask how their teeth help them survive and meet their needs.

Journal: Make a Book Show what you found out. In your book, also:
- Draw pictures of animals and what they eat.
- Make up and solve addition problems about animals and what they eat.

Name _____

Review What You Know

Vocabulary

1. Circle the problem that shows a **double**.

    $5 + 5 = 10$

    $5 + 6 = 11$

    $5 + 7 = 12$

2. Circle the word that tells which strategy can be used to add the numbers.

    $7 + 8 = ?$

    doubles

    near doubles

    count back

3. Circle the **sum** in the problem below.

    $7 + 4 = 11$

Addition and Subtraction

4. Robin has 9 stamps. Joe gives her 4 stamps. How many stamps does Robin have now?

    _____ stamps

5. Jen has 18 treats for her cat. She feeds some treats to her cat. Jen has 9 treats left. How many treats did Jen give her cat?

    _____ treats

Doubles Facts

6. Solve this doubles fact.

    $7 + 7 =$ _____

My Word Cards

Study the words on the front of the card. Complete the activity on the back.

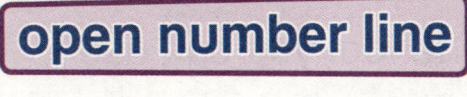

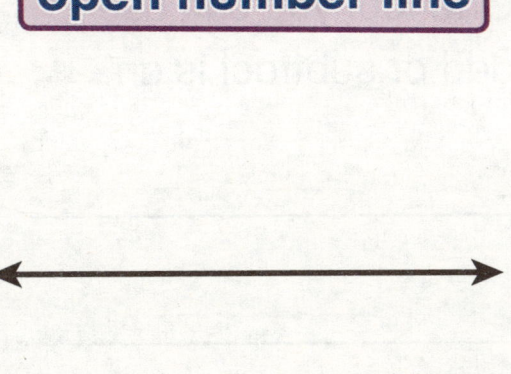

open number line

doubles-plus-1 fact

the addends are 1 apart

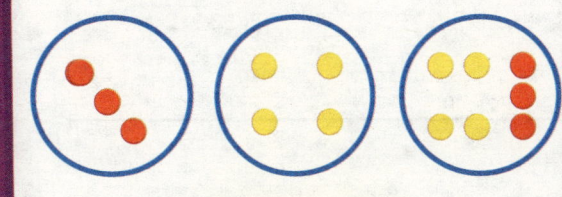

3 + 4 = 7
addends

doubles-plus-2 fact

the addends are 2 apart

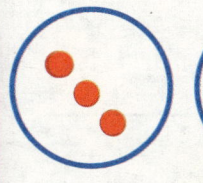

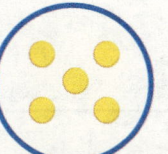

3 + 5 = 8
addends

My Word Cards

Use what you know to complete the sentences.
Extend learning by writing your own sentence using each word.

When adding numbers that are 2 apart, you can use a

_____

_____.

When adding numbers that are 1 apart, you can use a

_____

_____.

One tool you can use to add or subtract is an

_____

_____.

Name _____

Lesson 3-1
Count On to Add

Solve & Share

Abby has 5 cubes.
Salina gives her 7 more cubes.
How many cubes does Abby have now?
Show your thinking on the number line below.

I can ...
count on to add using a number line.

I can also model with math.

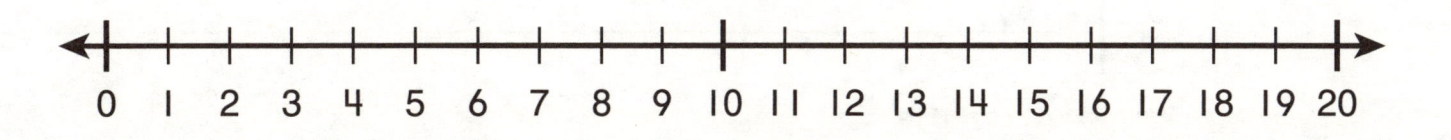

⬅|—|—|—|—|—|—|—|—|—|—|—|—|—|—|—|—|—|—|—|—|➡
0 1 2 3 4 5 6 7 8 9 10 11 12 13 14 15 16 17 18 19 20

____ cubes

Topic 3 | Lesson 1   one hundred fifty-five   **155**

Solve **7 + 8 = ?** using a number line.

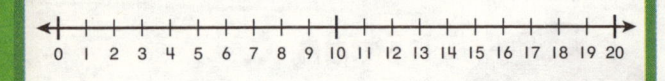

This number line has numbers from 0 to 20.

Find 7 on the number line. Then count on 8 more to add 7 + 8.

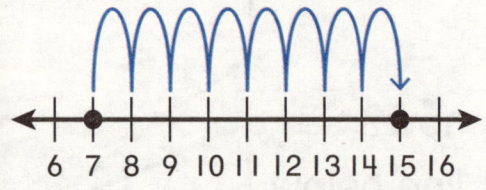

Start at 7 and make 8 jumps. You land on 15.

So, 7 + 8 = 15.

If you start at 8 and make 7 jumps, you land on the same number.

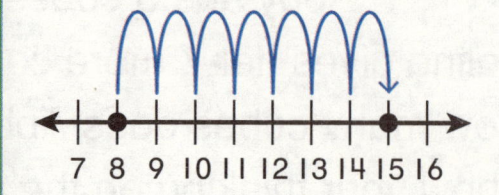

So, 8 + 7 = 15 too!

Do You Understand?

Show Me! How do you know where to start counting on? How do you know how many to count on?

Guided Practice Use the number line to count on and find each sum.

1. 9 + 7 = __16__

2. 9 + 9 = _____

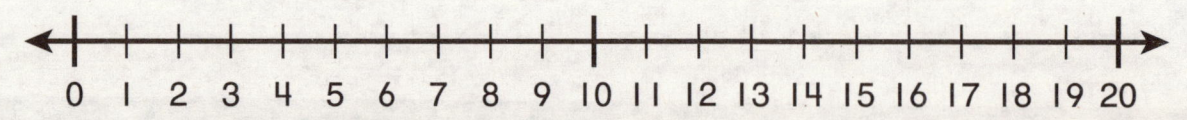

156 one hundred fifty-six

Topic 3 | Lesson 1

Name _____

Independent Practice Use a number line to count on and find each sum.

3. 7 + 4 = ____

4. 6 + 8 = ____

5. 9 + 4 = ____

6. 9 + 6 = ____

7. 7 + 7 = ____

8. 9 + 8 = ____

9. 6 + 4 = ____

10. 8 + 5 = ____

11. 3 + 9 = ____

Use a number line to count on to solve.

12. **Math and Science** Kim works at a zoo. She feeds the big cats 9 pounds of meat. She feeds the tortoises 7 pounds of leaves and berries.

How many pounds of food does Kim feed the animals?

____ pounds of food

Problem Solving Use a number line to solve the problems below.

13. **Reasoning** Scott walks 6 blocks. Then he walks 3 more blocks. Write the numbers that will help find out how many blocks Scott walked in all.

    6 + 3 = ___

    Start at ___.   Count on ___ more.

14. **Reasoning** Ramona mails 7 letters. Then she mails 8 more letters. Write the numbers that will help find out how many letters Ramona mailed in all.

    7 + 8 = ___

    Start at ___.   Count on ___ more.

15. **Higher Order Thinking** Write and solve a story problem. Show your work on a number line.

    _____
    _____
    _____   ___ + ___ = ___

16. ✓ **Assessment** Solve 5 + 9 = ? on the number line. Show your work.

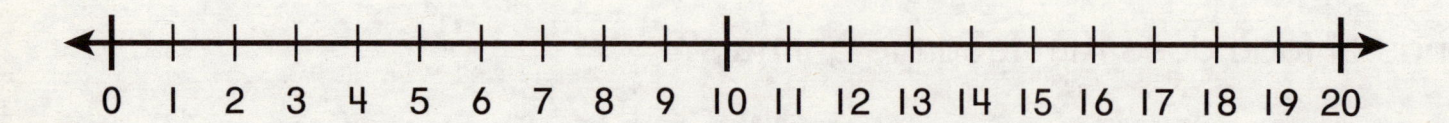

    0 1 2 3 4 5 6 7 8 9 10 11 12 13 14 15 16 17 18 19 20

Name _____

Homework & Practice 3-1
Count on to Add

Another Look! There is more than one way to count on to add 2 + 8.

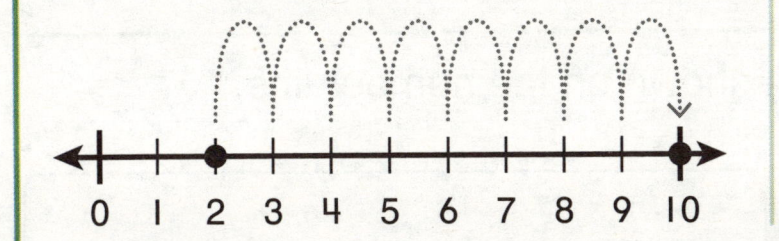

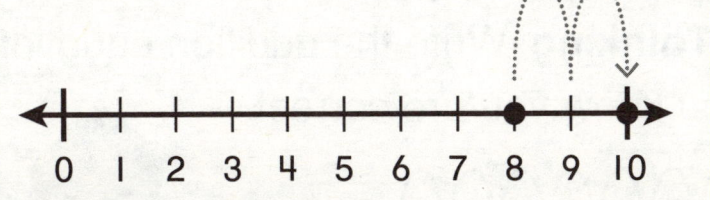

Start at 2, then take 8 jumps.

Start at 8, then take 2 jumps.

2 + 8 = 10

If you start at 8 instead of 2, you don't have to count on as many. Remember, you get the same answer both ways.

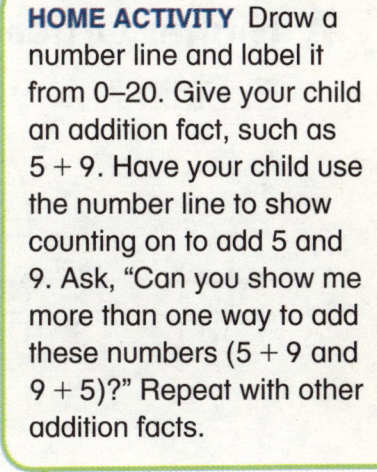

HOME ACTIVITY Draw a number line and label it from 0–20. Give your child an addition fact, such as 5 + 9. Have your child use the number line to show counting on to add 5 and 9. Ask, "Can you show me more than one way to add these numbers (5 + 9 and 9 + 5)?" Repeat with other addition facts.

Use a number line to count on and find each sum.

1. 9 + 4 = ___

2. 4 + 8 = ___

3. 9 + 7 = ___

Topic 3 | Lesson 1

Use a number line to count on and find each sum.

4. 9 + 6 = ____

5. 7 + 4 = ____

6. 8 + 5 = ____

7. **Higher Order Thinking** Write the addition equation shown on the number line. Explain how you know you are correct.

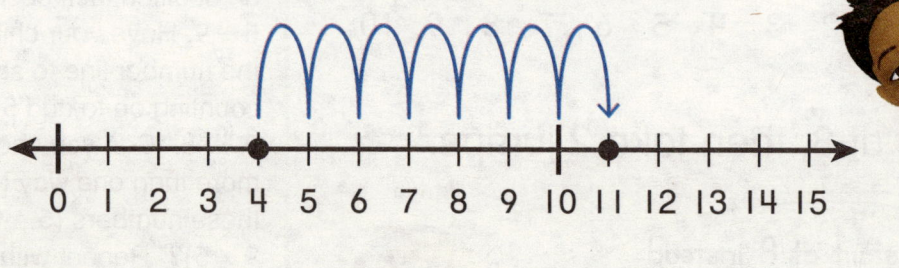

____ + ____ = ____

8. **Assessment** Daryl showed an equation on the number line below. Which of the following could be Daryl's equation?

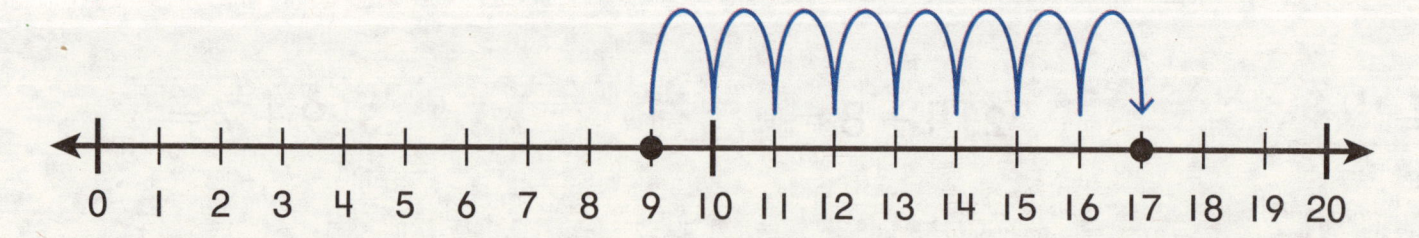

Ⓐ 9 + 9 = 18   Ⓑ 7 + 10 = 17   Ⓒ 9 + 8 = 17   Ⓓ 10 + 7 = 17

Name _____

Lesson 3-2
Count On to Add Using an Open Number Line

Arnie runs 8 miles on Thursday. He runs 9 more miles on Friday. How many miles did Arnie run in all? Use the number line to show how you know.

I can ...
count on to add using an open number line.

I can also make math arguments.

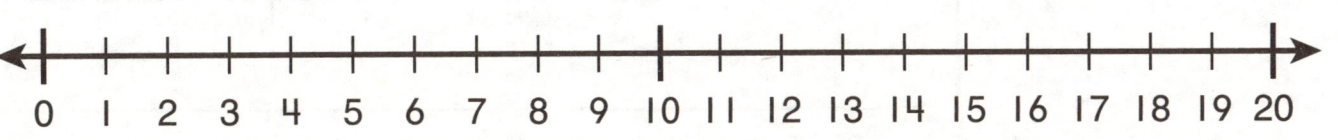

0 1 2 3 4 5 6 7 8 9 10 11 12 13 14 15 16 17 18 19 20

_____ miles

Topic 3 | Lesson 2

An **open number line** can help you add.

$7 + 6 = ?$

7

Start by placing the 7 on the number line.

Counting on by 1s is one way to add 6 more. Start at 7. Then count on 6 more.

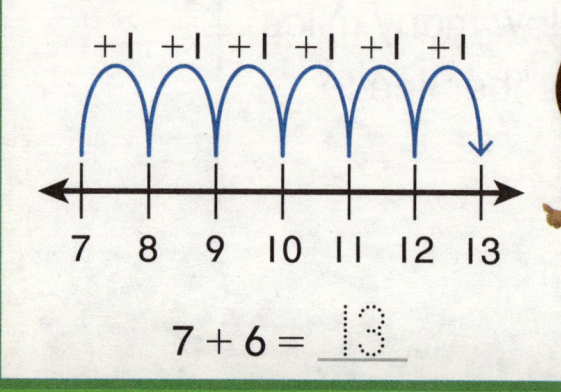

+1 +1 +1 +1 +1 +1

7 8 9 10 11 12 13

$7 + 6 = \underline{13}$

You can also break apart the 6. Adding 3 and 3 is one way to add 6 more.

+3   +3

7   10   13

$7 + 3 + 3 = \underline{13}$

I get the same sum no matter how I add.

Do You Understand?

Show Me! What number is always included on an open number line?

Guided Practice

Use the open number line to solve the problems. Show your work.

1. $7 + 5 = \underline{12}$

+3   +2

7   10   12

2. $6 + 2 = \underline{}$

162 one hundred sixty-two

Topic 3 | Lesson 2

Name _____

Independent Practice
Use the open number line to solve each problem. Show your work.

3. 4 + 7 = ____

⟵——————⟶

4. 8 + 8 = ____

⟵——————⟶

5. 6 + 6 = ____

⟵——————⟶

6. 9 + 7 = ____

⟵——————⟶

7. **Vocabulary** Solve the problem. Show your work on the **open number line** below.

8 + 6 = ____

⟵——————⟶

Think about what numbers to include on your number line.

Topic 3 | Lesson 2

Problem Solving

Use an open number line to solve each problem.

8. Use Tools Marco rides his bike 7 miles. Then he rides 9 more miles. How many miles did Marco ride in all?

____ + ____ = ____

____ miles

9. Use Tools Ana reads 10 books in January. She reads 10 books in February. How many books did Ana read in all?

____ + ____ = ____

____ books

10. Higher Order Thinking Kate has 8 roses. She picks some more roses. Now Kate has 17 roses. How many roses did Kate pick? Use words or pictures to explain how you know.

11. Assessment Solve the equation. Show your work on the open number line below.

9 + 6 = ____

164 one hundred sixty-four

Name _____

Homework & Practice 3-2
Count On to Add Using an Open Number Line

Another Look! You can count on to solve addition problems using an open number line.

8 + 9 = ?

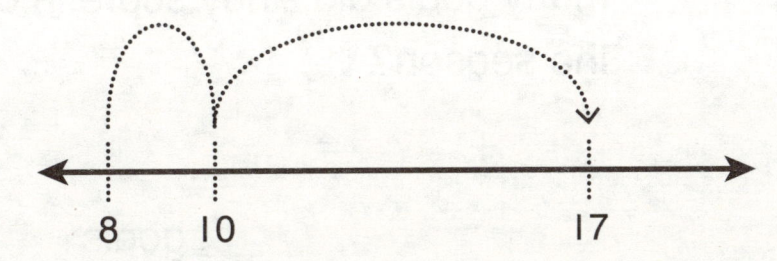

Start at __8__ and count on __9__ more.

8 + 9 = __17__

HOME ACTIVITY Draw an open number line. Give your child an addition fact, such as 6 + 8. Ask, "Which number can you put at the beginning of the number line?" Have him or her show 2 different ways to add 8 to 6. Repeat with different addition facts.

Use the open number line to solve the problems. Show your work.

1. 8 + 4 = ____

2. 8 + 7 = ____

Topic 3 | Lesson 2

Use an open number line to solve the problems.

3. Laura reads 8 pages on Monday. She reads 6 pages on Tuesday. How many pages did Laura read in all?

____ + ____ = ____

____ pages

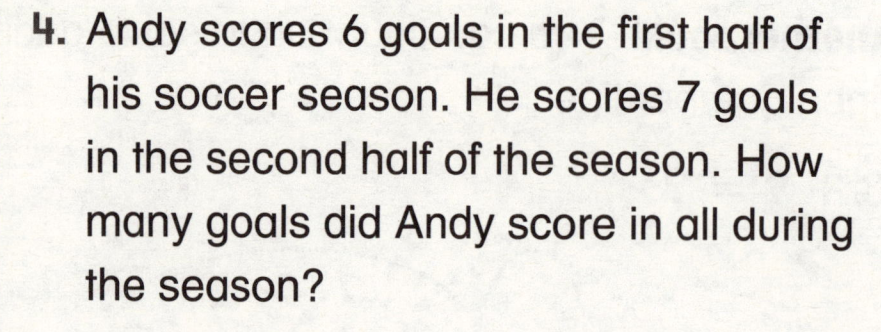

How many pages did Laura read on both Monday and Tuesday?

4. Andy scores 6 goals in the first half of his soccer season. He scores 7 goals in the second half of the season. How many goals did Andy score in all during the season?

____ + ____ = ____

____ goals

5. **Higher Order Thinking** Sam has 9 stamps in his collection. He gets some more. Now he has 18 stamps. How many more stamps did Sam get? Use words or pictures to show how you know.

6. **Assessment** Solve the equation. Show your work on the open number line below.

5 + 7 = ____

Name _____

Solve & Share

Carlos and Alisa each have 6 books. If they put their books together, how many books will they have in all? Show your thinking below.

Lesson 3-3
Doubles

I can ...
memorize doubles facts.

I can also model with math.

___ + ___ = ___

Topic 3 | Lesson 3 | Digital Resources at SavvasRealize.com | one hundred sixty-seven **167**

Let's look at some doubles facts that you may know.

$3 + 3 = 6$
$5 + 5 = 10$

Here are ways we can show these facts.

$3 + 3 = 6 \quad 5 + 5 = 10$

You can represent the doubles fact $6 + 6$ the same way.

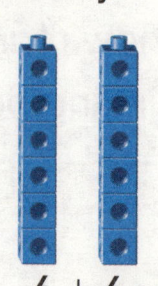

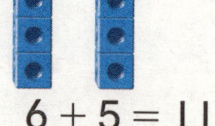

$6 + 6 = 12$

This isn't a doubles fact.

$6 + 5 = 11$

Do You Understand?

Show Me! Becca shows $6 + 7$ with cubes and says it is not a doubles fact. Is she correct? How do you know?

☆ Guided Practice ☆

Decide if each set of cubes shows a doubles fact. Circle your answer. Then write an equation to match the cubes.

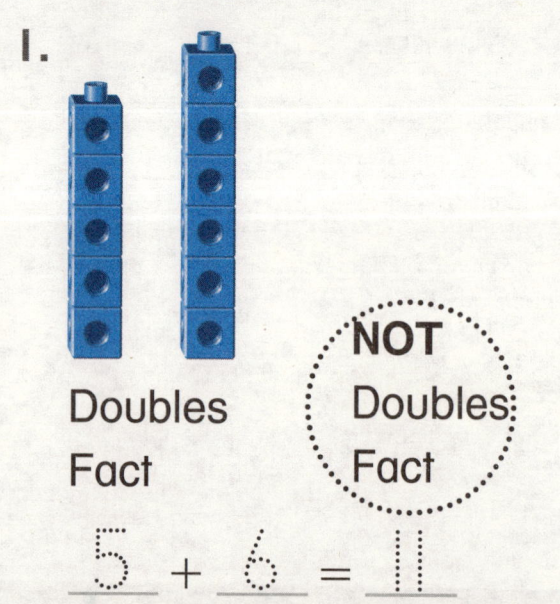

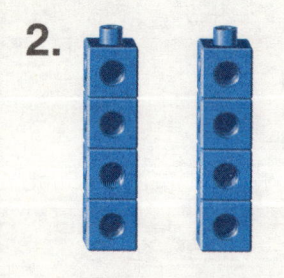

1. Doubles Fact   (**NOT** Doubles Fact)

$5 + 6 = 11$

2. Doubles Fact   **NOT** Doubles Fact

___ + ___ = ___

168 one hundred sixty-eight

Topic 3 | Lesson 3

Name _____

Independent Practice

Decide if each set of cubes shows a doubles fact. Circle your answer. Then write an equation to match the cubes.

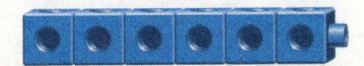

3.

Doubles Fact   **NOT** Doubles Fact   ___ + ___ = ___

4.

Doubles Fact   **NOT** Doubles Fact   ___ + ___ = ___

5.

Doubles Fact   **NOT** Doubles Fact   ___ + ___ = ___

6.

Doubles Fact   **NOT** Doubles Fact   ___ + ___ = ___

Complete each doubles fact.

7. $0 + 0 =$ ☐

8. ☐ $= 9 + 9$

9. $8 + 8 =$ ☐

10. $5 + 5 =$ ☐

Topic 3 | Lesson 3

Problem Solving

Use cubes to help you solve each number story.

11. Make Sense Andrew and his sister each pick 10 flowers. How many flowers did they pick in all?

Write an equation to match the problem.

___ + ___ = ___

___ flowers

12. Make Sense Pearl and Charlie each get 5 books for their birthday. How many books did they get in all?

Write an equation to match the problem.

___ + ___ = ___

___ books

13. Higher Order Thinking Max plays in 2 hockey games. He scores the same number of goals in each game. He scores 8 goals in all. How many goals did Max score in each game? Show your work below. Then write the equation you used to solve the problem.

___ = ___ + ___

14. Assessment Carrie takes the same number of pictures on both Saturday and Sunday. Which equations show the number of pictures Carrie could have taken? Choose all that apply.

☐ 7 + 7 = 14

☐ 8 + 6 = 14

☐ 8 + 8 = 16

☐ 9 + 7 = 16

Use cubes to help if you need to!

Name _____

Homework & Practice 3-3
Doubles

Another Look! Some facts are doubles facts. Some facts are not.

This is not a doubles fact.   This is a doubles fact.

"The addends are not the same."

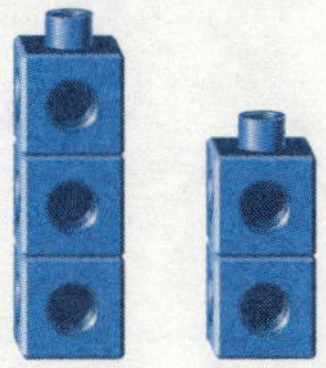

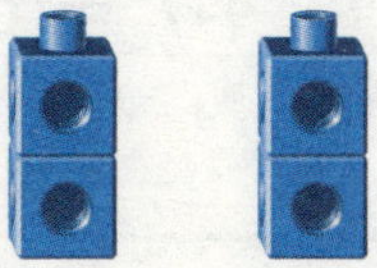

"In a doubles fact, both addends are the same."

$3 + 2 = \underline{5}$ $2 + 2 = \underline{4}$

HOME ACTIVITY Divide a strip of paper into 6–10 parts so that it looks like a cube tower. Ask your child to count the parts. Then cut the strip in half vertically so you have 2 strips each with 6–10 parts. Ask your child how many are in each tower. Have him or her tell you the doubles fact that is represented. Repeat with other numbers (1–10).

Decide if each set of cubes shows a doubles fact. Circle your answer. Then write an equation to match the cubes.

1. Doubles Fact   **NOT** Doubles Fact

   ___ + ___ = ___

2. Doubles Fact   **NOT** Doubles Fact

   ___ + ___ = ___

Topic 3 | Lesson 3   one hundred seventy-one **171**

Solve each fact. Circle the doubles. Use cubes if you need to.

3. ___ = 8 + 5

4. 5 + 5 = ___

5. 9 + 5 = ___

6. 10 + 10 = ___

7. ___ = 7 + 6

8. ___ = 9 + 9

9. 8 + 8 = ___

10. ___ = 3 + 4

11. 7 + 7 = ___

12. **Higher Order Thinking** Simone built the same number of model cars and model airplanes. Show how Simone could have built 14 models. Explain how you know.

13. ✓ **Assessment** Mike picks the same number of red apples and green apples. How many apples could Mike have picked? Choose all that apply.

☐ 19
☐ 18
☐ 17
☐ 16

Name _____

Lesson 3-4
Doubles Plus 1

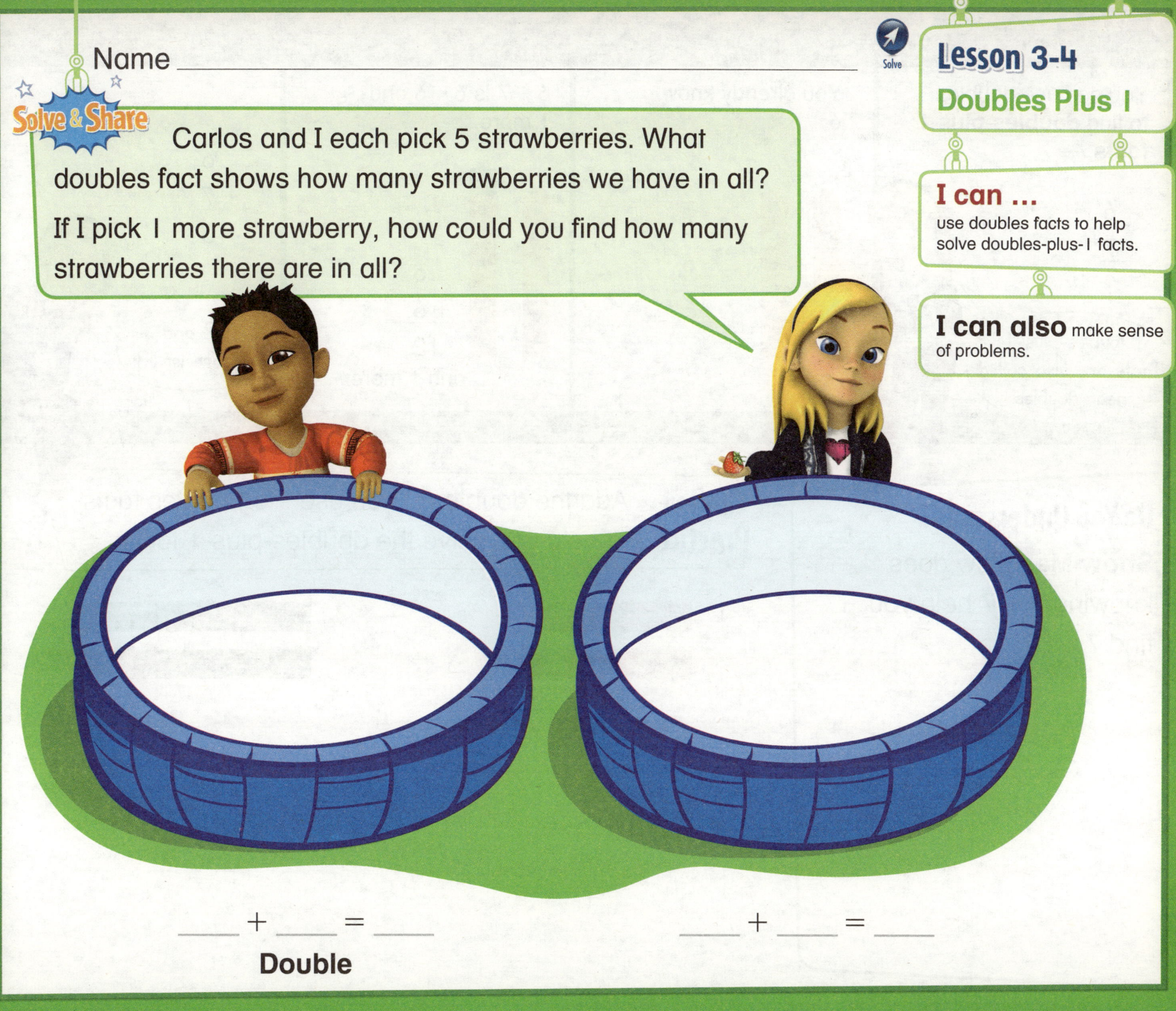

Solve & Share

Carlos and I each pick 5 strawberries. What doubles fact shows how many strawberries we have in all?

If I pick 1 more strawberry, how could you find how many strawberries there are in all?

I can ...
use doubles facts to help solve doubles-plus-1 facts.

I can also make sense of problems.

___ + ___ = ___
Double

___ + ___ = ___

Topic 3 | Lesson 4 Digital Resources at SavvasRealize.com one hundred seventy-three **173**

You can use doubles to find **doubles-plus-1 facts**.

6
+7

?

Doubles-plus-1 facts are also called near doubles.

You already know 6 + 6.

6
+6

12

6 + 7 is 6 + 6 and 1 more.

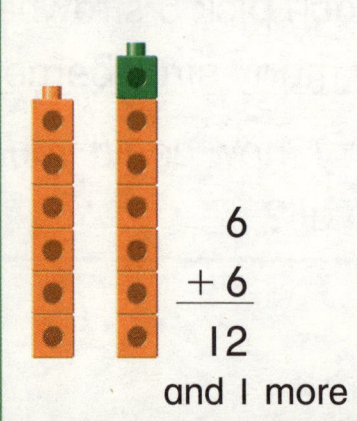

6
+6

12
and 1 more

6
+7

13

12 and 1 more is 13.

Do You Understand?

Show Me! How does knowing 7 + 7 help you find 7 + 8?

Guided Practice

Add the doubles. Then use the doubles facts to help you solve the doubles-plus-1 facts.

1. $5 + 5 = 10$

   So, $5 + 6 = 11$.

2. ___ + ___ = ___

   So, $8 + 9 = $ ___.

174 one hundred seventy-four

Topic 3 | Lesson 4

Name _____

Independent Practice

Add the doubles. Then use the doubles facts to help you solve the doubles-plus-1 facts.

3. 7   8
   +7   +7
   ☐   ☐

4. 4   4
   +4   +5
   ☐   ☐

5. 5   5
   +5   +6
   ☐   ☐

6. 9   9
   +9   +10
   ☐   ☐

7. 6   6
   +6   +7
   ☐   ☐

8. 3   3
   +3   +4
   ☐   ☐

Use a doubles-plus-1 fact to help you write an equation for the problem. Then draw a picture to show your work.

9. **Higher Order Thinking** Max has some blue marbles. Tom has some red marbles. Tom has 1 more marble than Max. How many marbles do they have in all?

___ + ___ = ___

Topic 3 | Lesson 4

one hundred seventy-five 175

Problem Solving Solve each problem below.

10. Reasoning Carrie and Pete each pick 7 cherries. Then Pete picks 1 more. How many cherries do they have in all?

Write an equation to match the problem.

___ + ___ = ___

___ cherries

11. Reasoning Manny and Pam each buy 5 apples. Then Pam buys 1 more. How many apples do they have in all?

Write an equation to match the problem.

___ + ___ = ___

___ apples

12. Higher Order Thinking Laura has to solve 9 + 8. Explain how she could use 8 + 8 to find the sum.

_____
_____
_____
_____

13. Assessment Juan eats 8 grapes after lunch. Then he eats some more grapes after dinner. He ate 17 grapes in all. How many grapes did Juan eat after dinner?

Ⓐ 8
Ⓑ 9
Ⓒ 7
Ⓓ 1

You can use doubles and a doubles-plus-1 fact to help you solve the problem.

Name _____

Homework & Practice 3-4
Doubles Plus 1

Another Look! You can use doubles facts to solve doubles-plus-1 facts.

$4 + 5 = ?$

$5 = 4 + 1$, so you can write $4 + 5$ as $4 + 4 + 1$.

$4 + 4$ | $+ 1$

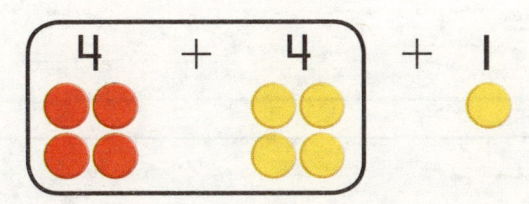

$4 + 4 = 8$

8 and 1 more is 9. So, $4 + 5 = 9$.

$2 + 3 = ?$

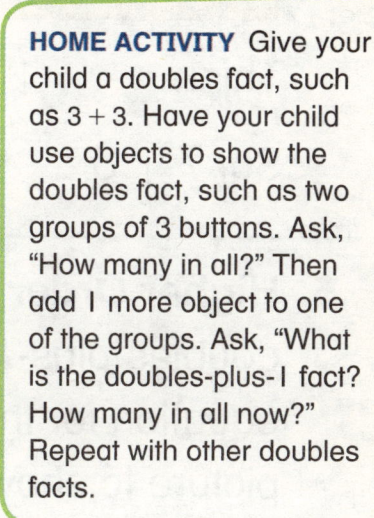

$3 = \underline{2} + \underline{1}$

$2 + 2$ | $+ 1$

$\underline{2} + \underline{2} = \underline{4}$

So, $\underline{2} + \underline{3} = \underline{5}$.

HOME ACTIVITY Give your child a doubles fact, such as 3 + 3. Have your child use objects to show the doubles fact, such as two groups of 3 buttons. Ask, "How many in all?" Then add 1 more object to one of the groups. Ask, "What is the doubles-plus-1 fact? How many in all now?" Repeat with other doubles facts.

Add the doubles. Then use the doubles facts to help you solve the doubles-plus-1 facts.

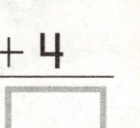

1. $\begin{array}{r} 3 \\ +3 \\ \hline \square \end{array}$ $\begin{array}{r} 3 \\ +4 \\ \hline \square \end{array}$

2. $\begin{array}{r} 6 \\ +6 \\ \hline \square \end{array}$ $\begin{array}{r} 6 \\ +7 \\ \hline \square \end{array}$

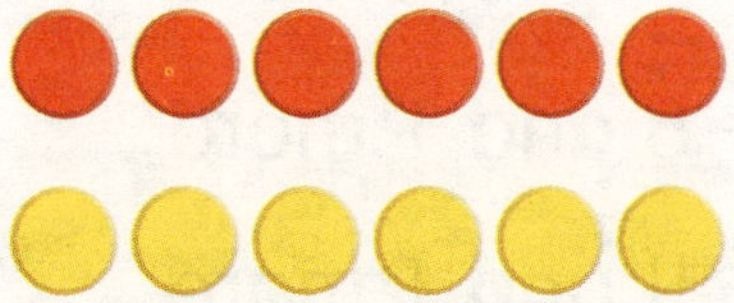

Draw 1 more cube. Use a doubles fact to help you add.

3. Think: ___ + ___ = ___.

So, 7 + 8 = ___.

4. Think: ___ + ___ = ___.

So, 9 + 10 = ___.

5. **Higher Order Thinking** Use a doubles-plus-1 fact to help you write an equation for the problem. Then draw a picture to show your work.

Dan saw some cats and dogs.
He saw 1 more dog than cat.
How many dogs and cats did Dan see?

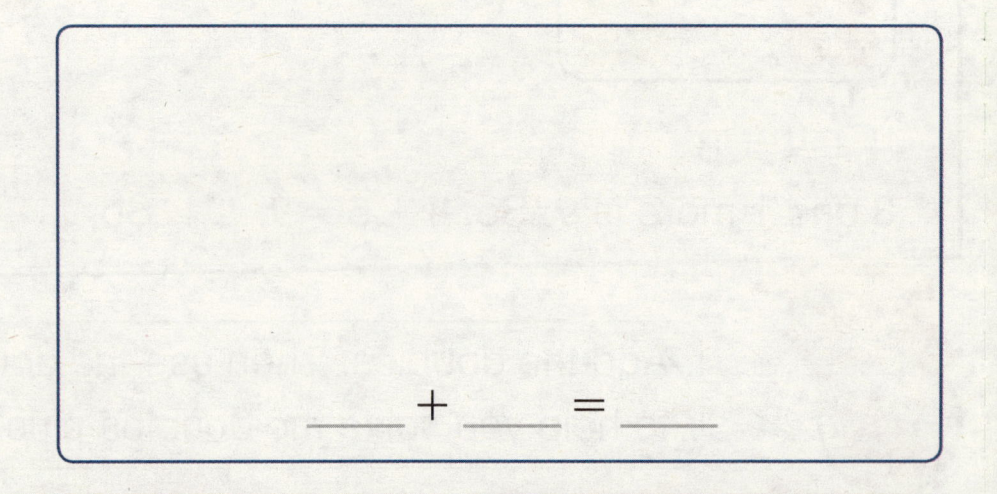

___ + ___ = ___

6. **Assessment** Which doubles-plus-1 fact should you use to solve 9 + 8?

Ⓐ 7 + 7 and 1 more
Ⓑ 8 + 8 and 1 more
Ⓒ 6 + 6 and 1 more
Ⓓ 9 + 9 and 1 more

7. **Assessment** Which doubles-plus-1 fact should you use to solve 5 + 6?

Ⓐ 6 + 6 and 1 more
Ⓑ 4 + 5 and 1 more
Ⓒ 5 + 5 and 1 more
Ⓓ 4 + 4 and 1 more

Name _____

Solve & Share

Carlos and I each find 5 seashells. What doubles fact shows how many seashells we have in all?

If Carlos finds 2 more seashells, how could you find how many seashells there are in all?

Lesson 3-5
Doubles Plus 2

I can ...
use doubles facts to help solve doubles-plus-2 facts.

I can also reason about math.

____ + ____ = ____   ____ + ____ = ____

Double

Topic 3 | Lesson 5 | one hundred seventy-nine **179**

These are called **doubles-plus-2 facts**.

$$\begin{array}{r} 6 \\ +8 \\ \hline ? \end{array} \qquad \begin{array}{r} 9 \\ +7 \\ \hline ? \end{array}$$

Doubles-plus-2 facts are also called near doubles.

There are different ways to solve a doubles-plus-2 fact.

$$\begin{array}{r} 6 \\ +8 \\ \hline ? \end{array}$$

Double the lesser number. Then add 2.

Think $6 + 6 = 12$ and 2 more.

Double 6 is 12. 2 more than 12 is 14.

$6 + 8 = 14$

Or, double the number between.

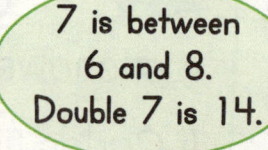

7 is between 6 and 8. Double 7 is 14.

Do You Understand?

Show Me! Which doubles facts can help you solve $7 + 9$? Explain.

☆ Guided Practice   Use the doubles fact to help you add.

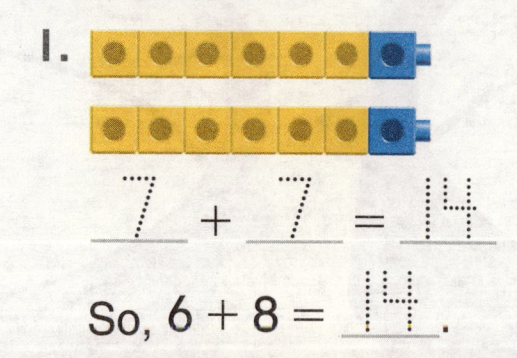

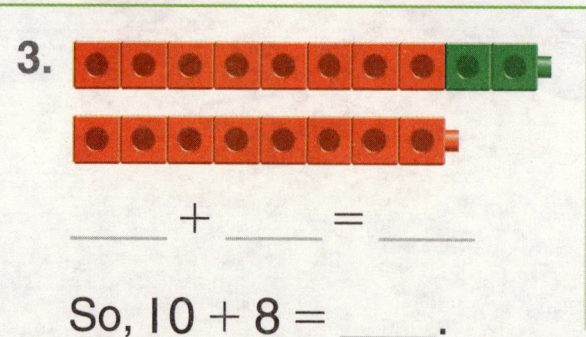

1. $\underline{7} + \underline{7} = \underline{14}$

   So, $6 + 8 = \underline{14}$.

2. $\underline{} + \underline{} = \underline{}$

   So, $5 + 7 = \underline{}$.

3. $\underline{} + \underline{} = \underline{}$

   So, $10 + 8 = \underline{}$.

4. $\underline{} + \underline{} = \underline{}$

   So, $7 + 9 = \underline{}$.

Name _____

Independent Practice

Draw 2 more cubes. Use a doubles fact to help you add.

5. ___ + ___ = ___

So, 10 + 8 = ___.

6. ___ + ___ = ___

So, 9 + 11 = ___.

7. ___ + ___ = ___

So, 8 + 6 = ___.

8. ___ + ___ = ___

So, 7 + 5 = ___.

9. ___ + ___ = ___

So, 4 + 6 = ___.

10. ___ + ___ = ___

So, 3 + 5 = ___.

Use a doubles or a doubles-plus-2 fact to help you write an equation for the problem. Draw cubes to help you.

11. **Number Sense** Dan makes a red cube train. Kay makes a yellow cube train. Kay's train has 2 more cubes than Dan's train. How many cubes do they have in all?

___ = ___ + ___

Problem Solving Solve each problem below.

12. Reasoning Kelly and Eric each make 6 sand castles. Then Kelly makes 2 more. How many sand castles did the two friends make in all?

Write an addition equation.

____ + ____ = ____

____ sand castles

13. Reasoning Mark finds 8 shells. Sue finds 2 more than Mark. Together, they find 18 shells. How many shells did Sue collect?

Write an addition equation.

8   ?

____ + ____ = ____

Sue collected ____ shells.

14. Higher Order Thinking Use a doubles-plus-2 fact to help you write an equation for the problem. Then solve.

There are some fish in a pond. Some fish are silver. Some fish are gold. There are 2 more gold fish than silver fish. How many fish are there in all?

____ + ____ = ____

silver   gold   fish
fish   fish

15. Assessment Ben sees 7 crabs. Jamie sees 9 crabs. How many crabs did they see in all?

Which should you use to find how many crabs Ben and Jamie saw in all?

Ⓐ 7 + 7 and 1 more

Ⓑ 7 + 9 and 1 more

Ⓒ 7 + 7 and 2 more

Ⓓ 9 + 9 and 2 more

182 one hundred eighty-two   Topic 3 | Lesson 5

Homework & Practice 3-5
Doubles Plus 2

Another Look! You can use doubles facts to solve doubles-plus-2 facts.

6 + 8 = ?

8 = 6 + 2, so you can write
6 + 8 as 6 + 6 + 2.

6 + 6 = 12
12 and 2 more is 14. So, 6 + 8 = 14.

2 + 4 = ?
4 = __2__ + __2__

__2__ + __2__ = __4__

So, __2__ + __4__ = __6__.

HOME ACTIVITY Give your child a doubles fact, such as 4 + 4. Have your child use objects to show the doubles fact, such as two groups of 4 paper clips. Ask, "How many in all?" Then add 2 more paper clips to one of the groups. Ask, "What is the doubles-plus-2 fact? How many in all now?" Repeat with other doubles facts.

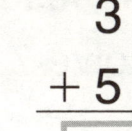

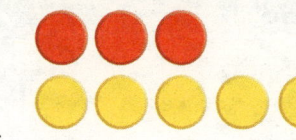

Add the doubles. Then use the doubles to help you solve the doubles-plus-2 facts.

1. 3   3
   +3   +5
   ☐   ☐

2. 4   6
   +4   +4
   ☐   ☐

Topic 3 | Lesson 5

one hundred eighty-three 183

Draw 2 more cubes. Then use the doubles to help you solve the doubles-plus-2 facts.

3.

Think: ____ + ____ = ____.
So, 5 + 7 = ____.

4.

Think: ____ + ____ = ____.
So, 3 + 5 = ____.

5. **Higher Order Thinking** Use a doubles-plus-2 fact to help you write an equation for the problem. Then draw a picture to show your work.

Tanya and Kyle feed the same number of birds at the zoo. Then Kyle feeds 2 more birds. How many birds did they feed in all?

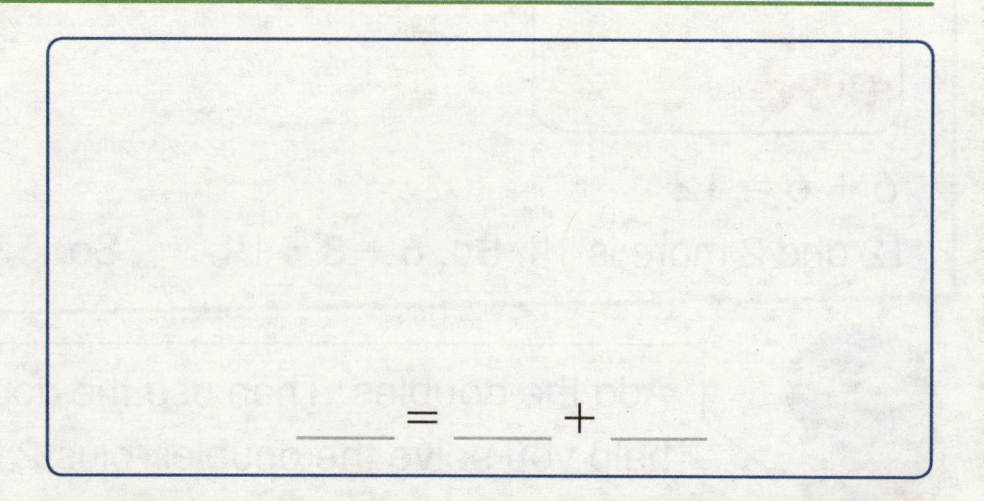

____ = ____ + ____

6. **Assessment** Max's team scores 8 runs on Monday and 10 runs on Tuesday. How many runs did the team score in all?

Which doubles fact will help you solve the problem?

Ⓐ 7 + 7
Ⓑ 6 + 6
Ⓒ 9 + 9
Ⓓ 10 + 10

7. **Assessment** Which should you use to solve 7 + 9?

Ⓐ 7 + 7 and 1 more
Ⓑ 7 + 7 and 2 more
Ⓒ 8 + 8 and 1 more
Ⓓ 8 + 8 and 2 more

Name _____

Lesson 3-6
Make 10 to Add

Solve & Share

How can thinking about 10 help you find the answer to the addition fact 9 + 5? Show your work and explain.

I can ...
make 10 to add numbers to 20.

I can also make math arguments.

____ + ____ = ____

Topic 3 | Lesson 6 · one hundred eighty-five **185**

Make 10 to help you add.

$$\begin{array}{r}7\\+4\\\hline?\end{array}$$

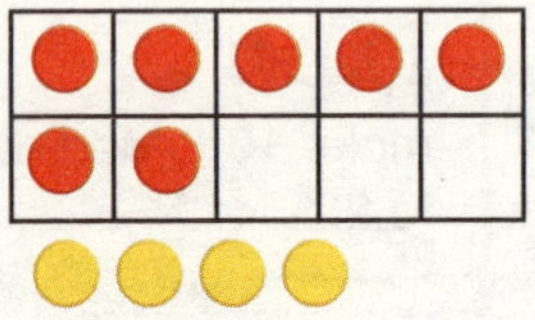

Move 3 counters from the 4 to the 7.

Now I have 10 and 1.

10 + 1 is the same as 7 + 4.

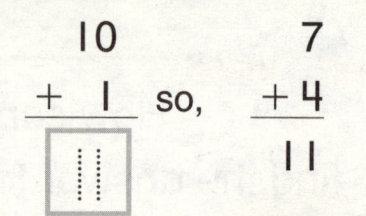

$$\begin{array}{r}10\\+1\\\hline\boxed{11}\end{array}$$

$$\begin{array}{r}10\\+1\\\hline\boxed{11}\end{array} \text{ so, } \begin{array}{r}7\\+4\\\hline 11\end{array}$$

The sums are the same!

Do You Understand?

Show Me! How would you make 10 to find the sum of 9 + 4?

☆ Guided Practice ☆

Draw counters to make 10. Then write the sums.

1. $\begin{array}{r}7\\+6\\\hline?\end{array}$

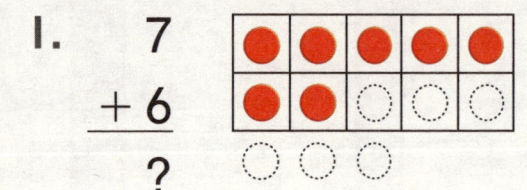

$\begin{array}{r}10\\+3\\\hline\boxed{13}\end{array}$ so, $\begin{array}{r}7\\+6\\\hline\boxed{}\end{array}$

2. $\begin{array}{r}8\\+6\\\hline?\end{array}$

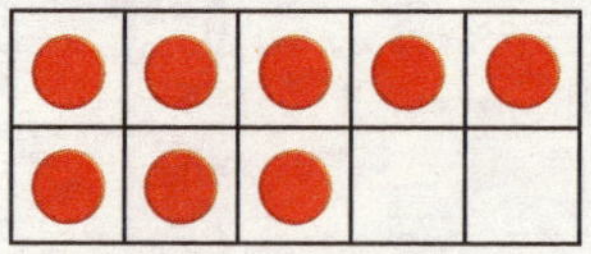

$\begin{array}{r}10\\+4\\\hline\boxed{}\end{array}$ so, $\begin{array}{r}8\\+6\\\hline\boxed{}\end{array}$

Name _____

Independent Practice

Draw counters to make 10. Then write the sums.

3. 7
   +8

    ?

   10   7
  + 5 so, +8
  ---   ---
  ☐   ☐

4. 9
   +6

    ?

   10   9
  + 5 so, +6
  ---   ---
  ☐   ☐

5. 7
   +7

    ?

   10   7
  + 4 so, +7
  ---   ---
  ☐   ☐

Draw counters to make 10. Use 2 different colors. Then write the sums.

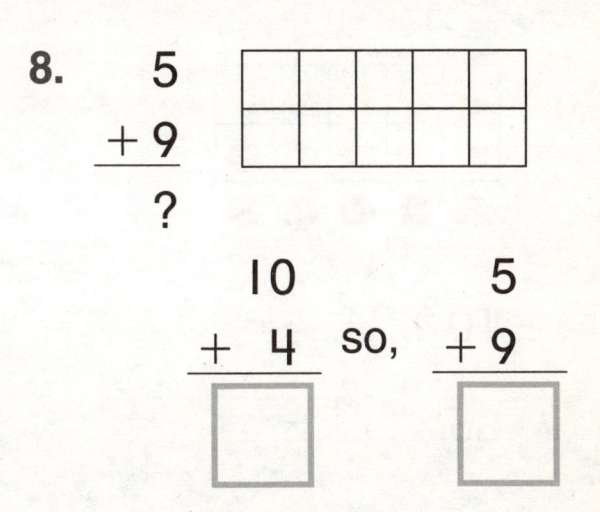

6. 4
   +8

    ?

   10   4
  + 2 so, +8
  ---   ---
  ☐   ☐

7. 6
   +5

    ?

   10   6
  + 1 so, +5
  ---   ---
  ☐   ☐

8. 5
   +9

    ?

   10   5
  + 4 so, +9
  ---   ---
  ☐   ☐

Problem Solving Draw counters to help you solve each problem below. Use 2 different colors.

9. **Model** Carlos sees 7 yellow birds in a tree. Then he sees 6 white birds in a tree. How many birds does Carlos see in all?

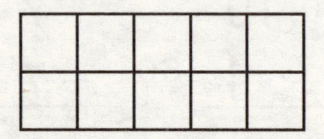

____ birds

10. **Model** Emily picks 8 red flowers. Then she picks 8 yellow flowers. How many flowers does Emily pick in all?

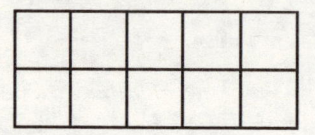

____ flowers

11. **Higher Order Thinking** Look at the model. Complete the equations to match what the model shows.

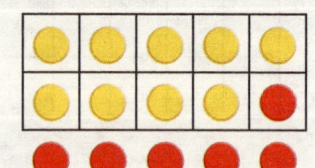

10 + ____ = ____

So, ____ + ____ = ____

12. **Assessment** Which number belongs in the ☐ ?

10 + 1 = 11

So, 6 + ☐ = 11

16   11   6   5
Ⓐ   Ⓑ   Ⓒ   Ⓓ

Homework & Practice 3-6
Make 10 to Add

Another Look! You can make 10 to help you add.

"7 and 5 more."

7 + 5 = ?

Make 10.

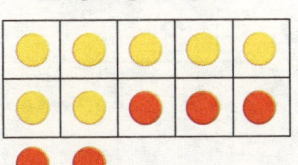

"10 and 2 more."

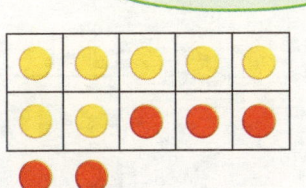

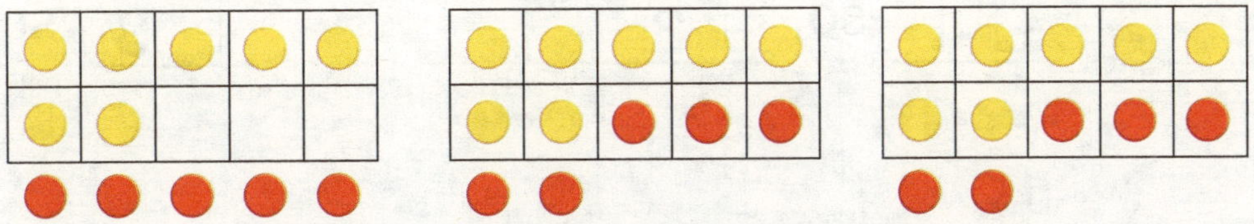

So, 7 + 5 and 10 + 2 have the same sum.

10 + 2 = __12__ so, 7 + 5 = __12__.

HOME ACTIVITY Have your child use small objects to show 7 + 6. Tell your child to move some objects to make 10. Then have your child give the 2 equations: 10 + 3 = 13 so, 7 + 6 = 13.

Draw counters to make 10. Then write the sums.

1. 9 + 6 = ?

   10 + 5   so,   9 + 6

2. 7 + 6 = ?

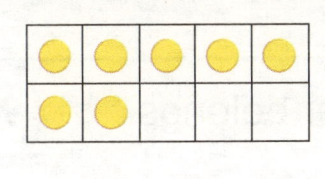

   10 + 3   so,   7 + 6

3. 5 + 6 = ?

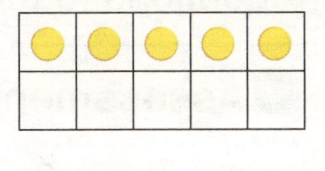

   10 + 1   so,   5 + 6

Topic 3 | Lesson 6

Draw counters to make 10. Use 2 different colors. Then write the sums.

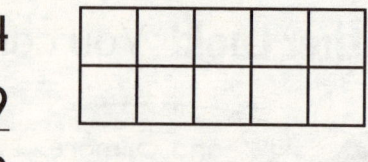

4. 9
   +5
   ___
    ?

   10   9
   + 4 so, +5
   ___   ___
   ☐   ☐

5. 8
   +3
   ___
    ?

   10   8
   + 1 so, +3
   ___   ___
   ☐   ☐

6. 4
   +9
   ___
    ?

   10   4
   + 3 so, +9
   ___   ___
   ☐   ☐

7. **Higher Order Thinking** Circle 2 numbers.

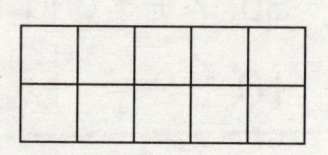

   5 6 7 8 9

   Draw counters to make 10 using the numbers circled. Use 2 different colors. Then write 2 addition equations to match.

   10 + ___ = ___.
   So, ___ + ___ = ___.

8. ✓**Assessment** Which number belongs in the ☐ ?

   9 + 6 = 15.
   So, 10 + ☐ = 15.

   9   5   6   8
   Ⓐ   Ⓑ   Ⓒ   Ⓓ

9. ✓**Assessment** Which number belongs in the ☐ ?

   8 + 5 = 13.
   So, ☐ + 3 = 13.

   7   8   9   10
   Ⓐ   Ⓑ   Ⓒ   Ⓓ

Name _____

Solve & Share

How can you make 10 to solve the addition fact 8 + 5? Show your work and explain.

Lesson 3-7

Continue to Make 10 to Add

I can ...
make 10 to add numbers to 20.

I can also make math arguments.

Make 10 to help you add.

$9 + 7 = ?$

9 is really close to 10. How can that help me find 9 + 7?

Think about the problem on a number line to help you make 10.

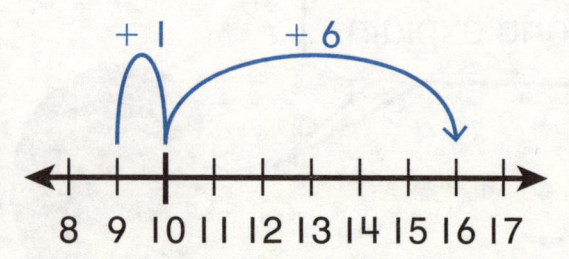

$+1$ $+6$

8 9 10 11 12 13 14 15 16 17

9 + 1 = 10 and 10 + 6 = 16.

You can think about $9 + 7$ as $9 + 1 + 6$, because $7 = 1 + 6$.

So, $9 + 7 = \underline{16}$

Do You Understand?

Show Me! How can you make 10 to find the sum of $7 + 6$?

Guided Practice

Make 10 find the sum. Use the number line to help you.

1. $\begin{array}{r} 8 \\ + 6 \\ \hline ? \end{array}$ $\begin{array}{r} 8 \\ + \boxed{2} \\ \hline 10 \end{array}$ $\begin{array}{r} 10 \\ + \boxed{4} \\ \hline \boxed{14} \end{array}$ so, $\begin{array}{r} 8 \\ + 6 \\ \hline \boxed{} \end{array}$

7 8 9 10 11 12 13 14 15 16 17 18 19 20

192 one hundred ninety-two

Copyright © Savvas Learning Company LLC. All Rights Reserved.

Topic 3 | Lesson 7

Name _____

Independent Practice — Make 10 to find the sum. Use a number line to help you.

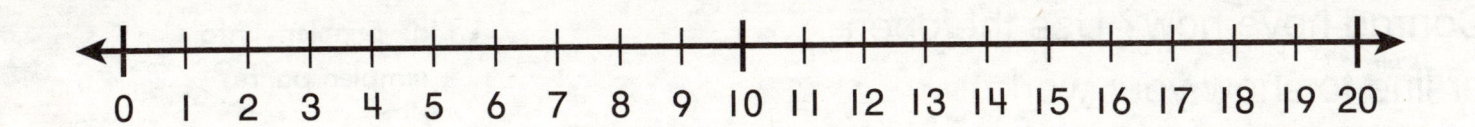

<--|--|--|--|--|--|--|--|--|--|--|--|--|--|--|--|--|--|--|--|-->
 0 1 2 3 4 5 6 7 8 9 10 11 12 13 14 15 16 17 18 19 20

2. 7   Think 7   10   7
   + 8   + ☐   + ☐   so, + 8
   ———   ———   ———   ———
    ?   10   ☐   ☐

3. 4   Think 4   10   4
   + 9   + ☐   + ☐   so, + 9
   ———   ———   ———   ———
    ?   10   ☐   ☐

4. 8   Think 10   8
   + 4   + ☐   so, + 4
   ———   ———   ———
    ?   ☐   ☐

5. 9   Think 10   9
   + 7   + ☐   so, + 7
   ———   ———   ———
    ?   ☐   ☐

6. 6   Think 10   6
   + 7   + ☐   so, + 7
   ———   ———   ———
    ?   ☐   ☐

7. **Number Sense** Jon adds 8 + 5. First, he adds 8 + 2 to make 10. What should he do next? _____

Topic 3 | Lesson 7

Problem Solving Make 10 to help you solve each number story.

8. **Look for Patterns** Conrad has 8 apples. Sam gives him 4 more. How many apples does Conrad have now? Use the open number line to show your work.

Can you break the problem into simpler parts?

Conrad has ____ apples.

9. **Higher Order Thinking** Pat makes 10 to solve 7 + 5 by changing the problem to 7 + 3 + 2. How does Pat make 10?

_____

_____

_____

10. **Assessment** Which shows how to make 10 to solve 9 + 6?

Ⓐ 9 + 4 + 2

Ⓑ 9 + 3 + 3

Ⓒ 9 + 1 + 5

Ⓓ 9 + 0 + 6

Name _____

Homework & Practice 3-7
Continue to Make 10 to Add

Another Look! You know how to add 10 to a number. So making 10 to add can be a helpful addition strategy.

$3 + 9 = ?$

You can break apart either addend to help you make 10.

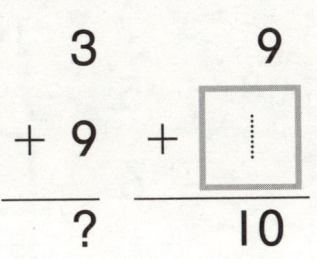

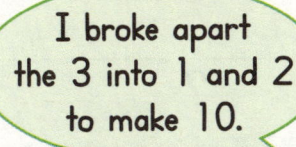

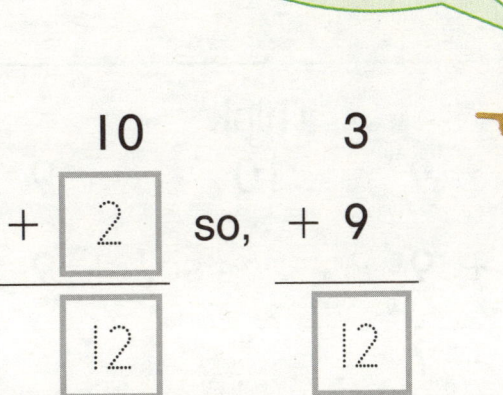

I broke apart the 3 into 1 and 2 to make 10.

```
  3       9       10          3
+ 9     + 1     + 2     so, + 9
---     ---     ---         ---
  ?      10      12          12
```

HOME ACTIVITY Start by reviewing with your child all the different ways to make 10 (e.g., 1 + 9, 2 + 8, etc.). Then give your child an addition fact with a sum from 11-19. Ask him or her to make 10 to add the two numbers. Repeat with different addition facts.

Fill in the missing numbers to solve each addition problem.

Think

1.
```
  9       9       10          9
+ 8     + □     + □     so, + 8
---     ---     ---         ---
  ?      10      □           □
```

Think

2.
```
  2       9       10          2
+ 9     + □     + □     so, + 9
---     ---     ---         ---
  ?      10      □           □
```

Topic 3 | Lesson 7   one hundred ninety-five **195**

Fill in the missing numbers to solve each addition problem.

3.
```
   7      Think        7
         10
 + 5    + ☐    so,  + 5
 ───    ───         ───
  ?      ☐           ☐
```

4.
```
   4      Think        4
         10
 + 9    + ☐    so,  + 9
 ───    ───         ───
  ?      ☐           ☐
```

5.
```
   8      Think        8
         10
 + 9    + ☐    so,  + 9
 ───    ───         ───
  ?      ☐           ☐
```

6.
```
   7      Think        7
         10
 + 8    + ☐    so,  + 8
 ───    ───         ───
  ?      ☐           ☐
```

7.
```
   9      Think        9
         10
 + 9    + ☐    so,  + 9
 ───    ───         ───
  ?      ☐           ☐
```

8.
```
   5      Think        5
         10
 + 6    + ☐    so,  + 6
 ───    ───         ───
  ?      ☐           ☐
```

9. **Higher Order Thinking** Jazmin says she can make 10 to solve 6 + 3. Is she correct? Explain how you know.

_____

_____

_____

10. ✓**Assessment** Which one shows how to make 10 to solve 8 + 8?

Ⓐ 8 + 8 + 2 = 8 + 10 = 18

Ⓑ 8 + 2 + 6 = 10 + 6 = 16

Ⓒ 8 + 1 + 8 = 9 + 10 = 19

Ⓓ 8 + 5 + 4 = 8 + 9 = 17

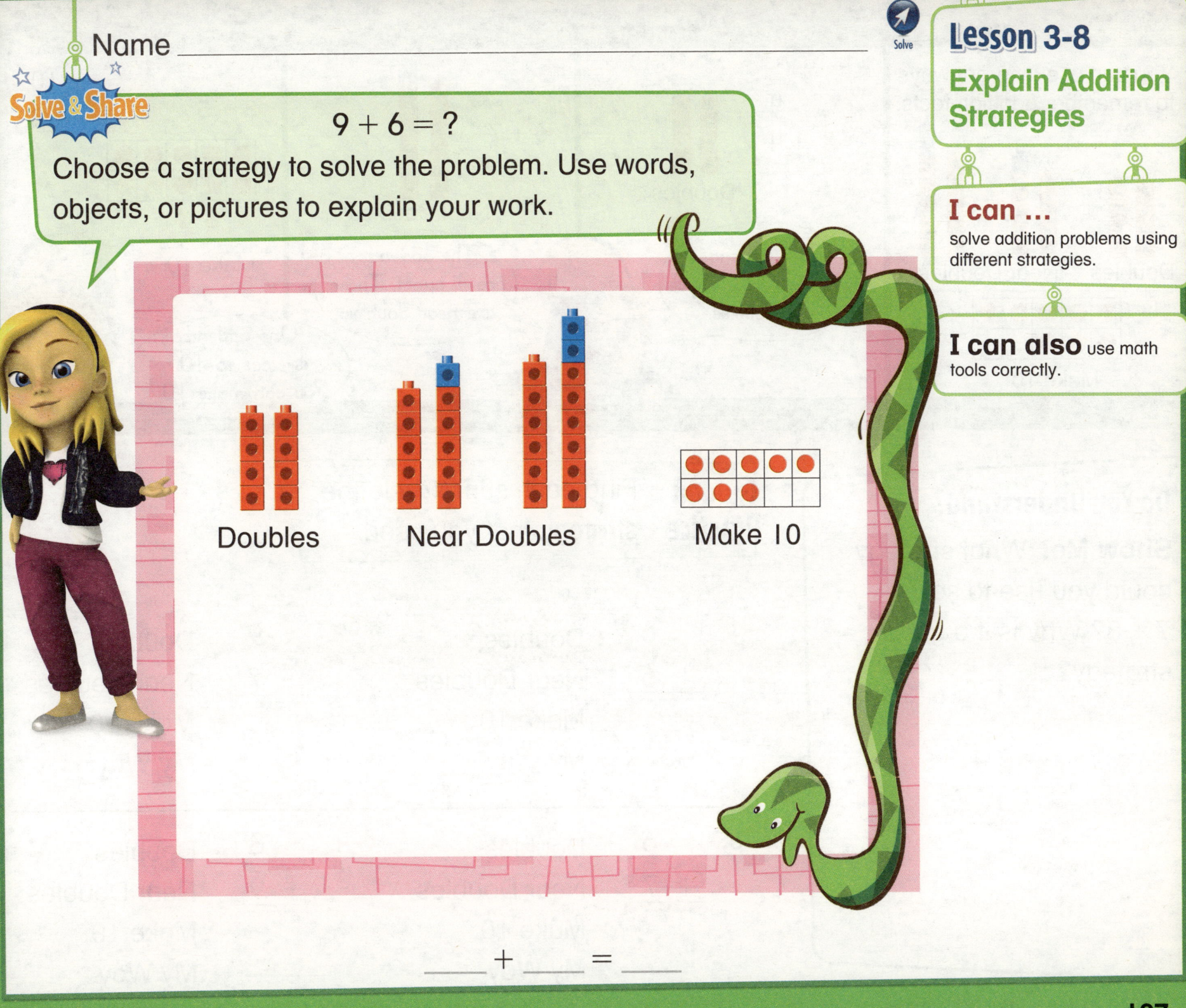

Name _____

Solve & Share

$9 + 6 = ?$

Choose a strategy to solve the problem. Use words, objects, or pictures to explain your work.

Doubles   Near Doubles   Make 10

____ + ____ = ____

Lesson 3-8
Explain Addition Strategies

I can ...
solve addition problems using different strategies.

I can also use math tools correctly.

Topic 3 | Lesson 8

one hundred ninety-seven **197**

You can use different ways to remember addition facts.

Doubles   Near Doubles

Make 10

$\begin{array}{r}4\\+4\\\hline\end{array}$

Doubles

"Both addends are the same. These are doubles."

$6 + 7$

Near Doubles

"The addends are 1 apart. These are near doubles."

$8 + 5$

$\begin{array}{r}10\\+3\\\hline\end{array}$

Make 10

"One addend is close to 10. You can make 10."

Do You Understand?

Show Me! What strategy could you use to solve $7 + 8$? Why is it a good strategy?

Guided Practice

Find each sum. Circle the strategy that you used.

1. $\begin{array}{r}6\\+6\\\hline 12\end{array}$ (Doubles) Near Doubles Make 10 My Way

2. $\begin{array}{r}9\\+7\\\hline\ \end{array}$ Doubles Near Doubles Make 10 My Way

3. $\begin{array}{r}6\\+7\\\hline\ \end{array}$ Doubles Near Doubles Make 10 My Way

4. $\begin{array}{r}8\\+9\\\hline\ \end{array}$ Doubles Near Doubles Make 10 My Way

Name _____

Independent Practice Find each sum.

5. 6
   +8
   ☐

6. 8
   +8
   ☐

7. 4
   +9
   ☐

8. 9
   +9
   ☐

9. 7
   +6
   ☐

10. 8
   +3
   ☐

11. 9
   +8
   ☐

12. 6
   +5
   ☐

13. 8
   +5
   ☐

14. 6
   +9
   ☐

15. 7
   +4
   ☐

16. 7
   +7
   ☐

Find the missing number. Explain the strategy you used.

17. **Algebra** Jan has 9 green marbles and some red marbles. She has 11 marbles in all.

9 + ____ = 11

Jan has ____ red marbles.

Topic 3 | Lesson 8

Problem Solving Solve each problem below.

18. **Make Sense** Brett has 8 shirts in his closet. He puts more shirts in the dresser. Now he has 16 shirts. How many shirts did Brett put in the dresser?

Brett put ____ shirts in the dresser.

Circle the strategy you used to find the missing number.

Doubles   Near Doubles   Make 10   My Way

19. **Higher Order Thinking** Manuel and Jake have 13 pencils in all. How many pencils could each boy have?

Circle the strategy you used to choose the missing addends.

Draw a picture to help you solve the problem.

$13 = \_\_\_ + \_\_\_$

Doubles   Make 10
Near Doubles   My Way

20. **Assessment** Sara has 7 big books. She has 8 small books. Which strategies could help you find how many books Sara has in all? Choose all that apply.

Doubles   Near Doubles   Make 10   My Way
☐   ☐   ☐   ☐

Name _____

Homework & Practice 3-8
Explain Addition Strategies

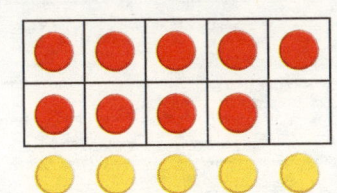

Another Look! You can use different strategies to solve problems.

5 and 6 are 1 apart. They are near doubles.

```
  5        5              5
+ 6      + 5            + 6
  ?       10             11
```

9 is close to 10. Make 10.

```
  9          10        9
+ 5         + 4  so  + 5
  ?          14       14
```

HOME ACTIVITY Have your child use small objects to show 8 + 9. Tell him or her to use one of the following strategies to find the sum: Doubles, Near Doubles, Make 10, or My Way. Ask your child to explain how he or she used that strategy to find the answer.

Find each sum. Circle the strategy that you used.

1.
```
  5
+ 7
```
Think: 5 and 7 are 2 apart.

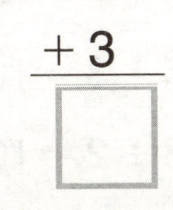

Doubles
Near Doubles
Make 10
My Way

2.
```
  8
+ 3
```
Think: 8 is close to 10.

Doubles
Near Doubles
Make 10
My Way

Topic 3 | Lesson 8

Find each sum. Circle the strategy that you used.

3. 9
   +3
   ☐
   Doubles
   Near Doubles
   Make 10
   My Way

4. 7
   +7
   ☐
   Doubles
   Near Doubles
   Make 10
   My Way

5. 7
   +9
   ☐
   Doubles
   Near Doubles
   Make 10
   My Way

6. **Higher Order Thinking** Write a story problem that can be solved by making 10. Then explain how to solve the problem.

7. ✓ **Assessment** Choose the equations that are **NOT** correct ways to solve the problem below by making 10. Choose all that apply.

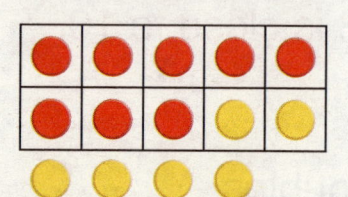

   ☐ $6 + 4 = 10; 10 + 0 = 10$

   ☐ $7 + 3 = 10; 10 + 1 = 11$

   ☐ $8 + 2 = 10; 10 + 4 = 14$

   ☐ $9 + 1 = 10; 10 + 3 = 13$

Name _____

Solve & Share

Caleb collects stickers. He has 4 more stickers than Zoe. Zoe has 5 stickers. How many stickers does Caleb have? Use objects, drawings, or an equation to show your thinking.

Lesson 3-9
Solve Addition Word Problems with Facts to 20

I can ...
solve different types of addition word problems.

I can also make math arguments.

Caleb has ____ stickers.

Topic 3 | Lesson 9

Tonya reads 5 books. She reads 7 fewer books than Seth. How many books did Seth read?

Tonya read 5 books. Tonya has read 7 fewer books than Seth.

This also means that Seth read 7 more books than Tonya.

What do you know?

What do you need to find out?

How many books Seth read

Seth read 7 more books than Tonya. So I need to add 5 + 7 to solve this problem.

To find out how many books Seth read, you can write an equation.

5 + 7 = 12

Seth read 12 books!

Do You Understand?

Show Me! Could you find out how many books Seth has by using objects or a drawing? Explain.

Guided Practice

Read the story. Then solve the problem with an equation.

1. Tim writes 9 stories. Tim writes 3 fewer stories than Daisy. How many stories did Daisy write?

   Tim writes [3] fewer stories than Daisy.

   Daisy writes [3] more stories than Tim.

   [9] [+] [3] = [ ]

2. Sherry reads 6 comic books. Dally reads 5 more comic books than Sherry. How many comic books did Dally read?

   Dally reads [ ] more comic books than Sherry.

   [ ] ◯ [ ] = [ ]

Name _____

Independent Practice — Solve the problems with objects, drawings, or an equation. Show your work.

3. Tracy buys 10 buttons on Monday.
   She buys more buttons on Tuesday.
   Now she has 19 buttons.
   How many buttons did Tracy buy on Tuesday?

   _____ buttons

4. Jen has 9 coins.
   Jen has 6 fewer coins than Owen.
   How many coins does Owen have?

   _____ coins

5. 14 cans are on the table.
   5 cans are big and the rest are small.
   How many small cans are on the table?

   _____ small cans

Topic 3 | Lesson 9

two hundred five **205**

Problem Solving Solve each problem below.

6. **Model** Leland cuts out 12 flowers. How many can he color red and how many can he color yellow?

Draw a picture and write an equation to model and solve the problem.

_____ red flowers   _____ yellow flowers

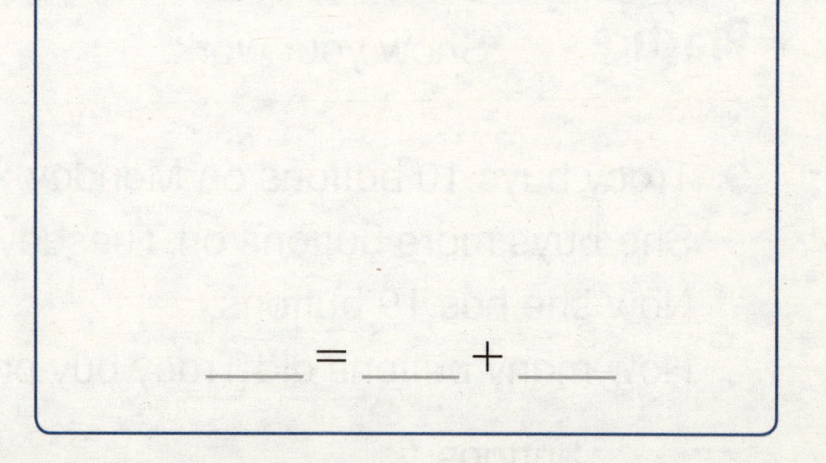

_____ = _____ + _____

7. **Higher Order Thinking** Nicole scored 8 goals this season. She scored 9 fewer goals than Julien. How many goals did Julien score?

Restate this problem using the word *more*.

Nicole scored 8 goals this season. Julien scored _____

_____

8. **Assessment** Dan drinks 6 more glasses of water than Becky. Becky drinks 5 glasses of water. How many glasses of water did Dan drink?

Which equation would you use to solve this problem?

Ⓐ $6 - 5 = 1$

Ⓑ $6 + 5 = 11$

Ⓒ $11 + 6 = 17$

Ⓓ $11 - 6 = 5$

Name _____

Homework & Practice 3-9
Solve Addition Word Problems with Facts to 20

Another Look! You can use counters and equations to solve problems.

Jake hits 8 baseballs.
He hits 5 fewer baseballs than Andy.
How many baseballs did Andy hit?

Jake hit 8 baseballs.

Jake hit 5 fewer baseballs than Andy.

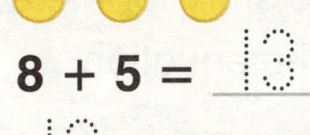

That means Andy hit 5 more baseballs than Jake.

8 + 5 = 13

Andy hit __13__ baseballs.

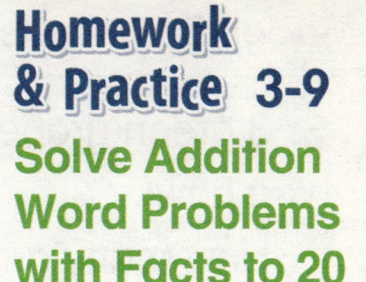

HOME ACTIVITY Tell your child a number story using either the word *more* or the word *fewer*. Then ask him or her to model the number story using counters and write an equation to solve. Sample story: "John has 4 sweaters. Chris has 5 more sweaters than John. How many sweaters does Chris have?" 4 + 5 = 9. Chris has 9 sweaters.

Draw counters and write equations to solve.

1. Maude sees 3 more foxes than Henry. Henry sees 4 foxes. How many foxes did Maude see?

   ___ + ___ = ___ foxes

2. Desiree has 2 fewer cards than Wendy. Desiree has 9 cards. How many cards does Wendy have?

   ___ + ___ = ___ cards

Topic 3 | Lesson 9

Model Draw a picture and write an equation to solve.

3. 3 green grapes and 10 red grapes are in a bowl.
How many grapes are in the bowl?

____ + ____ = ____   ____ grapes

4. 8 cats play. Some more cats come to play. 15 cats are playing now. How many cats came to play with the 8 cats?

____ + ____ = ____   ____ cats

5. **Higher Order Thinking** Complete the story for the equation below using the words **James**, **fewer**, and **Lily**. Then solve the equation.

$9 + 4 = ?$

James sees 4 _____ birds than Lily. _____ sees 9 birds. How many birds does _____ see?

____ + ____ = ____

6. **Assessment** Chad made 6 fewer sandwiches than Sarah. Chad made 7 sandwiches. How many sandwiches did Sarah make?

Which equation would you use to solve this problem?

$7 - 6 = 1$
Ⓐ

$7 - 1 = 6$
Ⓑ

$7 + 6 = 13$
Ⓒ

$6 + 10 = 16$
Ⓓ

Name _____

Solve & Share

A pet store has 9 frogs. 5 of the frogs are green and the rest are brown. Lidia adds 5 + 9 and says that the store has 14 brown frogs.

Circle if you **agree** or **do not agree** with Lidia's thinking. Use pictures, words, or equations to explain.

Agree   **Do Not Agree**

Problem Solving

Lesson 3-10
Critique Reasoning

I can ...
critique the thinking of others by using pictures, words, or equations.

I can also add and subtract correctly.

Thinking Habits
Can I improve on Lidia's thinking?

Are there mistakes in Lidia's thinking?

5 dogs are playing. Some more dogs join. Now 8 dogs are playing. Joe says 3 more dogs joined because $5 + 3 = 8$.

How can I decide if I agree or do not agree with Joe?

I can ask Joe questions, look for mistakes, or try to make his thinking clear to me.

I will draw a picture.

5 dogs some more dogs
8 dogs

$5 + 3 = 8$ dogs

I agree with Joe's thinking.

Do You Understand?

Show Me! What question would you ask Joe to have him explain his thinking?

Guided Practice

Circle your answer. Use pictures, words, or equations to explain.

1. 9 cats chase a ball. Some cats stop to eat. Now there are 4 cats chasing the ball.

   Stan says 13 cats stop to eat because $9 + 4 = 13$.
   Do you **agree** or **not agree** with Stan?

   Agree   Not Agree

Name _____

Independent Practice — Circle your answer. Use pictures, words, or equations to explain.

2. 14 grapes sit in a bowl. 9 are green. The rest are purple. How many are purple?

   Steve says 6 grapes are purple because $9 + 6 = 14$. Do you **agree** or **not agree** with Steve?

   Agree   **Not Agree**

3. 11 oranges are in a bag. 8 oranges fall out. How many oranges are left in the bag?

   Maria says 3 oranges are left because $11 - 3 = 8$. Do you **agree** or **not agree** with Maria?

   Agree   **Not Agree**

Topic 3 | Lesson 10

Problem Solving

Performance Assessment

Flower Vases Jill has 15 roses. She wants to put some in a red vase and some in a blue vase.

Jill solved the problem. Answer the items below to check her thinking. Use pictures, words, or equations to explain.

4. **Explain** Jill says she can put an equal number of roses in each vase. She says she can write a doubles fact to match the flowers in the blue and red vases. Do you agree? Explain.

5. **Model** How could Jill have used words or drawings to show the problem?

Name _____

Homework & Practice 3-10
Critique Reasoning

Another Look! Lidia has 10 pennies. Jon has 8 pennies. Sheila says Jon has 2 fewer pennies than Lidia because $10 - 8 = 2$.

Do you agree or not agree with Sheila?

Lidia ○○○○○○○○○○
Jon ○○○○○○○○
$10 - 8 = 2$

I used a picture and equation to show that Sheila is correct. Jon does have 2 fewer pennies than Lidia. I agree with Sheila.

HOME ACTIVITY Take turns writing your own addition problems involving single digit numbers. Show how you solved the problem using objects or pictures. Make mistakes in some of your problems and challenge each other to find the correct work and the mistakes.

Circle your answer. Use pictures, words, or equations to explain.

1. Anna says that $7 + 4$ is equal to $3 + 9$ because both are equal to 11. Do you **agree** or **not agree** with Anna?

   Agree   Not Agree

Topic 3 | Lesson 10

Performance Assessment

The Birds

9 birds land on a fence. Some more come. Now there are 18 birds on the fence. How many birds came to the fence?

Max solved the problem. Answer the items below to check his thinking. Use pictures, words, or equations to explain.

2. **Explain** Max says that he can use a doubles fact to solve this problem. Do you agree? Explain.

3. **Model** How could Max have used words or drawings to show the problem?

Name _____

Point & Tally

TOPIC 3 — **Fluency Practice Activity**

Find a partner. Get paper and a pencil.
Each partner chooses a different color: light blue or dark blue.

Partner 1 and Partner 2 each point to a black number at the same time. Both partners add those numbers.

If the answer is on your color, you get a tally mark.

Work until one partner gets twelve tally marks.

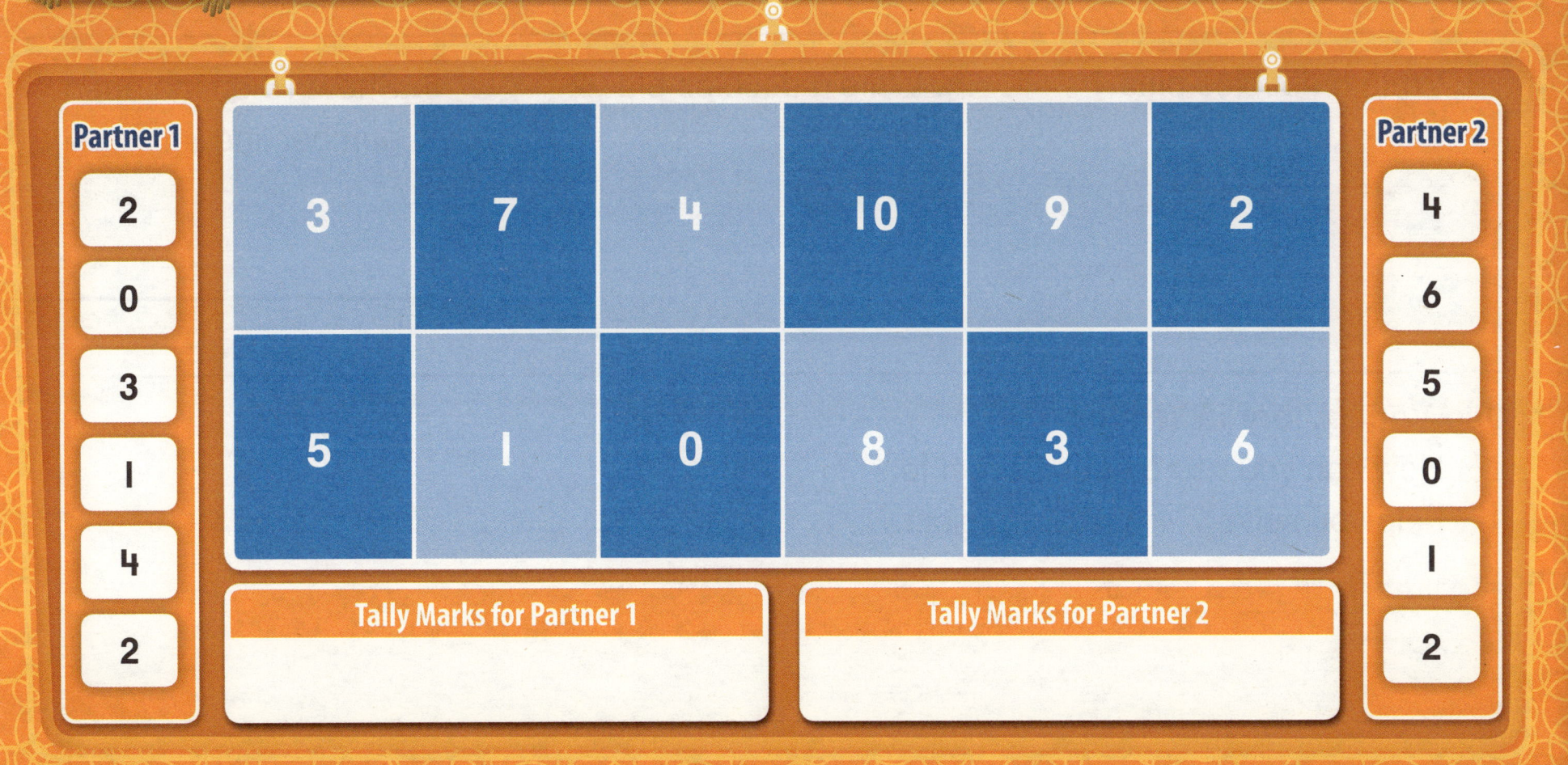

I can ...
add and subtract within 10.

Partner 1: 2, 0, 3, 1, 4, 2

3	7	4	10	9	2
5	1	0	8	3	6

Partner 2: 4, 6, 5, 0, 1, 2

Tally Marks for Partner 1

Tally Marks for Partner 2

Topic 3 | Fluency Practice Activity

Vocabulary Review

Word List
- doubles-plus-1 fact
- doubles-plus-2 fact
- open number line
- whole

Understand Vocabulary

1. Circle **True** or **False**.

    $10 + 5 = 15$ is a doubles-plus-1 fact.

    True   False

2. Circle **True** or **False**.

    In the equation below, 8 is the whole.

    $10 + 8 = 18$

    True   False

3. Write a doubles-plus-1 fact.

4. Write a doubles-plus-2 fact.

5. Show 15 on the open number line.

    ⟷

Use Vocabulary in Writing

6. How can you use a doubles fact to help you solve $7 + 8 = 15$. Explain.

Name _____

Set A

Reteaching

You can use an open number line to help solve an addition equation. Kara has 10 coins. She gets 8 more coins from her friend. How many coins does Kara have now?

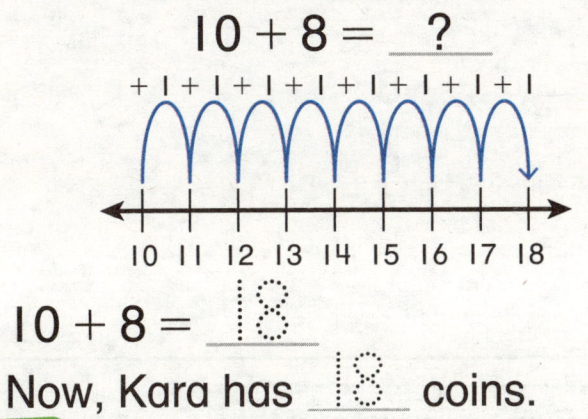

10 + 8 = ___?___

10 + 8 = __18__

Now, Kara has __18__ coins.

Use an open number line to solve the problem. Show your work.

1. Carmen recycles some cans on Monday. She recycles 4 cans on Tuesday. She recycles 13 cans in all. How many cans did Carmen recycle Monday?

_____ cans

Set B

A doubles-plus-1 fact is a doubles fact and 1 more.

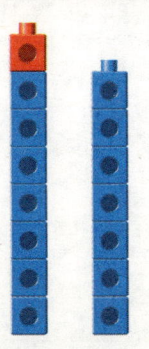

$$8 + 7 = ?$$

$$8 + 7 = 15$$

7 + 7 = 14.
14 and 1 more is 15.

Add the doubles. Then use the doubles fact to help you add 1 more.

2. 5 + 5 = ☐   6 + 5 = ☐

3. 8 + 8 = ☐   8 + 9 = ☐

Topic 3 | Reteaching

Set C

A doubles-plus-2 fact is a doubles fact and 2 more.

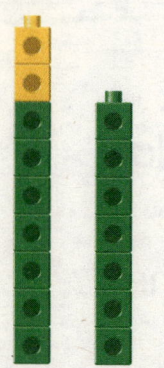

$$\begin{array}{r} 9 \\ +7 \\ \hline ? \end{array} \qquad \begin{array}{r} 9 \\ +7 \\ \hline 16 \end{array}$$

$7 + 7 = 14.$

14 and 2 more is 16.

Add the doubles. Then use the doubles fact to help you add 2 more.

4. $\begin{array}{r} 5 \\ +5 \\ \hline \end{array}$ $\begin{array}{r} 7 \\ +5 \\ \hline \end{array}$

5. $\begin{array}{r} 6 \\ +6 \\ \hline \end{array}$ $\begin{array}{r} 8 \\ +6 \\ \hline \end{array}$

Set D

You can make 10 to add.

$$\begin{array}{r} 8 \\ +6 \\ \hline ? \end{array}$$

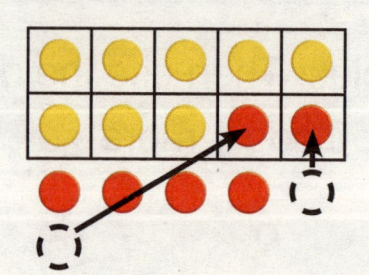

$\begin{array}{r} 10 \\ +4 \\ \hline 14 \end{array}$ so $\begin{array}{r} 8 \\ +6 \\ \hline 14 \end{array}$

Make 10 to add. Draw counters in the ten-frame to help you.

6. $\begin{array}{r} 7 \\ +8 \\ \hline ? \end{array}$

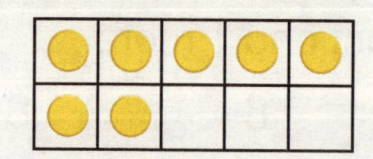

$\begin{array}{r} 10 \\ +5 \\ \hline \end{array}$ so $\begin{array}{r} 7 \\ +8 \\ \hline \end{array}$

Name _____

Set E

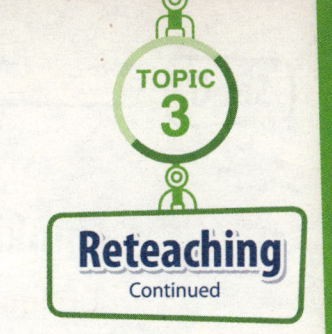

You can choose different ways to add.

Doubles   Near Doubles

Make 10

Find each sum. Circle the strategy that you used.

7. 8
   +4
   ☐

   Doubles   Make 10
   Near Doubles   My Way

8. 7
   +8
   ☐

   Doubles   Make 10
   Near Doubles   My Way

Reteaching Continued

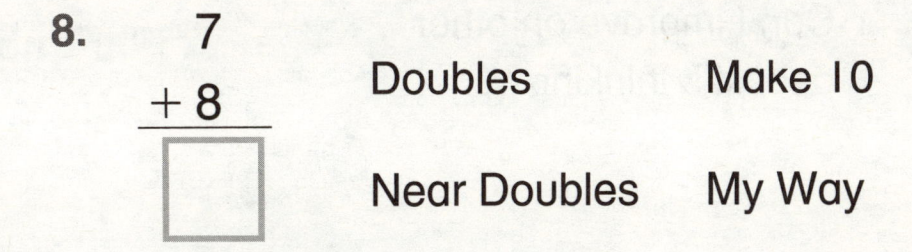

Set F

You can write an equation to help you solve addition problems.

Sean plays in 8 soccer matches. Kieran plays in 3 more matches than Sean. In how many matches does Kieran play?

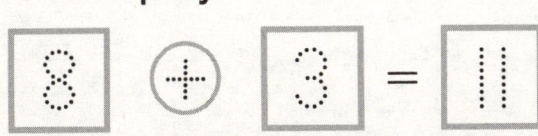

☐ 8 ☐ ⊕ ☐ 3 ☐ = ☐ 11 ☐

Kieran plays in __11__ soccer matches.

Write an equation to solve the problem.

9. Leslie has 8 pencils. She has 9 fewer pencils than Michelle. How many pencils does Michelle have?

☐ ◯ ☐ = ☐

Michelle has ____ pencils.

Topic 3 | Reteaching

two hundred nineteen 219

Set G

Thinking Habits
Critique Reasoning

What questions can I ask to understand other people's thinking?

Are there mistakes in other people's thinking?

Can I improve on other people's thinking?

Circle your answer. Use pictures, words, or equations to explain.

10. 6 books are on a shelf. Some more books are put on the shelf. Now there are 15 books on the shelf. How many books were put on the shelf?

    Kyle says that there were 9 books put on the shelf because $6 + 9 = 15$. Do you **agree** or **not agree** with Kyle?

    Agree   **Not Agree**

Name _____

1. Frank has 7 paper airplanes.
He makes 9 more.
How many paper airplanes does
Frank make in all?

- Ⓐ 18
- Ⓑ 17
- Ⓒ 16
- Ⓓ 15

2. Mark has 7 red marbles.
He has 8 blue marbles.
How many marbles does
Mark have in all?

- Ⓐ 14
- Ⓑ 15
- Ⓒ 16
- Ⓓ 17

3. Use the open number line. Show how to count on to find the sum.

$7 + 9 =$ _____

4. Is each addition fact below a doubles fact? Fill in the circle for **Yes** or **No**.

4 + 5 = 9   ○ Yes   ○ No

10 + 5 = 15   ○ Yes   ○ No

7 + 7 = 14   ○ Yes   ○ No

10 + 10 = 20   ○ Yes   ○ No

5. 8 birds are in a tree.
9 more birds join them.
How many birds are in the tree now?
Write an equation to solve the problem.

___ ○ ___ = ___ birds

6. Gloria has 7 yellow pencils. She has 9 red pencils. How many pencils does Gloria have in all? Choose all the strategies that could help you solve the problem.

☐ Doubles Plus 1

☐ Make 10

☐ Doubles Plus 2

☐ My Way

Think about the strategies you have learned!

Name _____

7. Nina bakes 8 corn muffins on Tuesday. She bakes 8 corn muffins on Wednesday. How many corn muffins does Nina bake in all?

Which number line shows the problem?

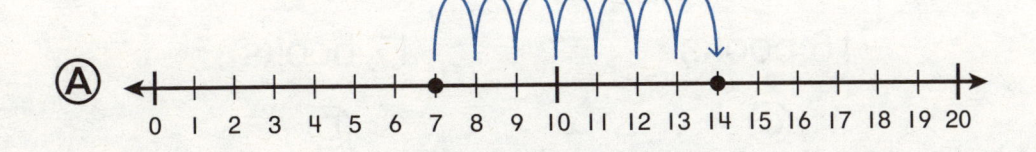

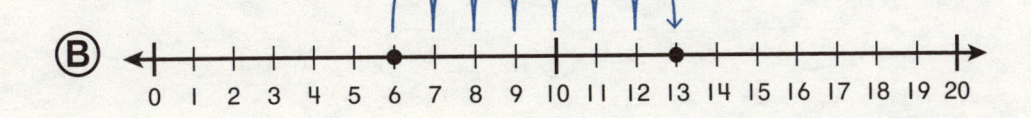

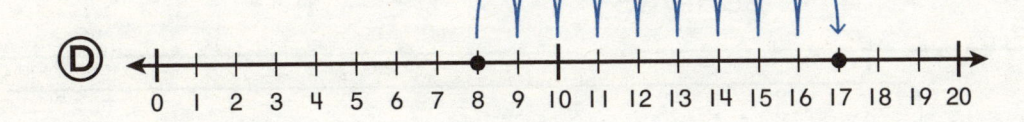

Ⓐ [number line 0–20 with jumps from 7 to 14]

Ⓑ [number line 0–20 with jumps from 6 to 13]

Ⓒ [number line 0–20 with jumps from 8 to 16]

Ⓓ [number line 0–20 with jumps from 8 to 17]

---

8. Sandy makes 9 bracelets. Then she makes 5 more bracelets. How many bracelets does Sandy have now?

Solve the problem. Explain the strategy you used.

9. Ming has 8 books.
   She buys 5 more books.
   How many books does
   she have in all?

   Make 10 to add.

   11 books   13 books   15 books   17 books
      Ⓐ   Ⓑ   Ⓒ   Ⓓ

10. Maria has 8 more scarves than Lucy.
    Lucy has 8 scarves.
    How many scarves does Maria have?
    Write an equation to solve.

    ___ + ___ = ___   ___ scarves

11. There were 19 limes on the table.
    10 fell to the floor. Nicky says there
    are 9 limes left on the table.

    Do you **agree** or **not agree** with
    Nicky's thinking? Use pictures, words,
    or equations to explain.

    Agree   **Not Agree**

Name _____

Roger's Reading Record

Roger loves to read!
The chart shows how many books he read for six months.

Roger's Reading	
Month	Number of Books
January	9
February	7
March	6
April	8
May	5
June	8

1. How many books did Roger read in all in April and June? Write an equation to solve.

   ____ + ____ = ____

   ____ books

2. Roger read 4 more books in July than he did in January. How many books did he read in July? Draw a picture to solve. Then write an equation to match.

   ____ + ____ = ____

   He read ____ books in July.

3. In February, Tracy and Roger read 15 books in all. How many books did Tracy read in February?

Explain the strategy that you used to solve the problem.

_____
_____
_____
_____

_____ books

4. Sharon read 8 books in March. She said that she read 2 fewer books than Roger in March.

Do you **agree** or **not agree** with Sharon? Circle your answer.

Use pictures, words, or equations to explain.

Agree   **Not Agree**